D1519709

Like a Swan on Water

My Journey to Defining My Unique Ethnic, Cultural, and Spiritual Identity

BARBARA G. PRATT

Like a Swan on Water
Copyright © 2024
Barbara G. Pratt

ISBN: 9798325605246

Library of Congress Cataloging in Publication Data Pratt, Barbara
TXu002414103
1-13482794866

Connect with us at:

instagram.com/likeaswanonwater

facebook.com/groups/likeaswanonwater

This book is dedicated to my late mother,
Fujiko Kaneko Lee, the strongest woman I've ever known.
In more ways than I can count, she was my greatest
inspiration.
Two weeks after I completed this manuscript, Mom passed
away peacefully in her sleep.

Rest well Mom - You deserve it.

Barbara G. Pratt

Contents

Prologue

I recall the exact day I knew I had to share my story. I'd always promised myself I'd write a book, but it was on this day that the universe gave me the sign that writing a book was not an "if," but a "when."

The memory of that day is so clear. Just after all Hell had broken loose, I publicly shared my reaction to a situation that had just occurred in my life, on social media. It was after I had fallen apart and taken some time to regain my composure. I posted my reflection on social media a week later.

The response to my post overwhelmed me. In less than a day, I'd received an unprecedented number of messages from friends, family, and followers. Women and men alike sent virtual hugs, messages of gratitude, and encouraging words applauding my courage in sharing. What struck me as funny was that I hadn't even revealed the actual situation that led to my writing the post. I had only lamented about life having "kicked my butt" that week before. I shared my very human reaction to it, and even wished out loud for some earth-shattering epiphany. But the truth was, there was none. At least not at that moment.

A few of my close male friends read my post and expressed their concerns. They feared that I was about to convey the stereotype of the angry Black female. Two of them called me within minutes of my posting, urging me to stop before things got out of hand. Having grown up with brothers, raised two sons, and worked in male-dominated environments, I knew what they feared—that I had shown vulnerability.

Posting on social media was not new to me, but this post was different from my usual upbeat, quirky, and funny posts.

The messages poured in at an unprecedented rate, and to this day, people still remember that one post and don't hesitate to remind me of it.

My message resonated with them.

After a few hours, I hid the post from my timeline. Although I initially appreciated the supportive messages, I grew uncomfortable with what I perceived as pity that people were now feeling for me. While I draw energy from nurturing others, accepting empathy or worse, sympathy, is difficult for me.

Every year, around the anniversary of that post, I revisit it and read the responses. The incident itself, though significant, is not germane to my story. I didn't share the details then, and they are equally unimportant now. Let's just say it was, as we would say in the old neighborhood, "jacked up."

My goal in telling my story is to share my unique journey that I hope will inspire, entertain and encourage readers. Writing this book has been both the easiest, and the hardest thing I've ever done. Because it was too hard to confront certain topics, I put down my laptop more times than I can count. Retelling stories often means reliving them.

Recounting the highlights has been great, but revisiting the lowest lows has been challenging, yet cathartic. In the day-to-day grind, it's important to remind ourselves of the things we've done to make a difference. Looking back on my experiences, I have come to deeply appreciate the lessons I derived from them.

They all led me to where I am today. I am a swan in the water, appearing to glide gracefully along. But just below the surface, my feet are flailing and flapping wildly and furiously.

My story is about venturing beneath the surface, beyond the facade, and sharing a version that very few know. As you join me on this journey, I hope you see me as a friend, sharing my personal stories, challenges and victories with you. Through hearing my experiences and the Monday-morning quarterbacking, I hope you will avoid some of my mistakes (and yes, there have been many), take positive shortcuts, and approach certain situations with more foresight and emotional intelligence than I had.

As writers often do, I have taken some creative license with the stories. Some names and timeframes have been changed to protect both the innocent and the guilty. But believe this. These stories are all true. If you know me personally, you may recognize yourself in some of my adventures. If you don't, I hope you still find flashes of yourselves in my stories and nod, thinking, "Yep, been there, done that." In other cases, I hope you see yourself in my shoes and self-reflect when you witness my silliness, awesomeness, and all the stuff in between.

No, there won't be exercises at the end of each chapter. The lessons are embedded in the stories, and I hope that as you reflect on them, you knead out the learnings that apply to you.

Proud of both my Asian and American ethnicities, I infuse references to my cultures throughout my story and explore their impacts on my life. A word of caution—some of the content made me uncomfortable, and I hope it does the same for you. It is within these areas of discomfort that most of my growth has occurred. Otherwise, it would be nothing more than a fairy tale with some wild turns. I don't pretend that my life bears much resemblance to a fairy tale, but I have experienced plenty of "fairy tale" moments.

Acknowledgements

There are so many people whom I need to thank for helping me to get this book out of my head, spirit, and heart, and onto paper and spoken word. There are too many to name here. There are many whom you'll meet as you follow along with me on my journey.

I must start by mentioning my amazing sons: Kendall and Brendan, to whom I gave birth. From the moment they entered the world, they reshaped my whole life, my reason for living, and my worldview.

I thank my late beautiful, incredible mother, who singlehandedly had the most profound effect on my life. I am eternally grateful to my beloved husband Michael, who continues to show me that fairy tales can and do come true. Deep gratitude goes to my best friend Tina. Because she has lived through a lot of it, Tina could probably write a good part of this story. I can't leave out my dear friend Kandii J. We met in our twenties, but I like to say we grew up together. I deeply love and thank my bonus children, Jeanine, Payton, and Christopher, and many others whom you'll meet along the way.

Embracing the Beauty of Human Flaws:
Kintsugi and the Art of Transformation

I am a Black Japanese woman who was born on an Air Force base in Santa Barbara, California. Growing up in inner-city Philadelphia, I received my education in the local public school system. With little assistance from my parents or anyone else, I navigated my way into college and earned my bachelor's degree. Soon thereafter, I pursued a master's degree. Among my work experience, I've worked for four prominent companies in the Philadelphia area. I am currently enjoying my second career as an entrepreneur, and now a writer.

I am in my second and last marriage, to Michael. From my first marriage, I have two amazing sons, ages twenty-seven and twenty-nine. When I married Michael, I gained the privilege of having two beautiful stepdaughters and a brilliant stepson. Together, Michael and I have five children whom we love and fiercely protect.

Throughout my journey, I have successfully navigated some of the most esteemed and high-performing companies. I have also achieved the "fairy tale" scenario of having not one, but two happy marriages, children, the house with the white picket fence, and even a cat. I have also made more mistakes along the way than I can count. It is through these missteps and errors that I have gained the most valuable lessons.

This is my story, and I am telling it from my unique perspective — because these are the only lenses through which I see life. My successes have been many. The more valuable lessons have been from the missteps and mistakes I've made. The foundation for my entire life's growth and resilience was built on my embracing of a simple Japanese principle, Kintsugi. I'm uncertain if there exists an American equivalent to this Japanese term.

Kintsugi is an artistic technique whereby broken or damaged ceramics are repaired or recreated using gold. Instead of aiming to restore the broken pottery to its original form, Kintsugi embraces the brokenness by exposing and sealing the cracks with a beautiful gold adhesive, resulting in a new and potentially even more amazing work of art. The mended fractures and repairs then become integral to the object's history and its inherent beauty.

Kintsugi grants us the power to redefine our hardships and challenges and encourages us to embrace the learnings and growth that emerge from those experiences. Drawing an analogy to life, the hope is that this restored and recreated piece symbolizes a more mindful and resilient "work of art."

I view my life as a dynamic piece of art. In American culture, we often attempt to hide, cover our flaws and imperfections, or simply get rid of them. Truth be told, I would have had a lot of covering up to do. Instead, I choose to wear my breaks and cracks as badges of honor. My kintsugi.

Let me begin by sharing one of my earliest childhood memories, which occurred one day as I was returning home from kindergarten.

Just as I did every school day after completing my half-day morning session of kindergarten, I walked the three blocks from Andrew Hamilton school in West Philly to my home, at fifty-sixth and Addison Street, alone. That's what five-year-old kindergarteners with two working parents did back then.

When I arrived at my house, I absent-mindedly climbed the stairs and went to open the door to our three-bedroom row home just as I'd done every school day. Except on this day, I returned home to a padlocked front door. Greeting me were signs with big letters affixed to the door. Multiple locks I was certain were not there when I left that morning prevented me from opening the normally unlocked door to my home. Believe it or not, I recall wondering why anyone would put the locks on the outside of the door like that!

Puzzled, I began ringing the doorbell. No answer. I rang the bell again. I'm not sure whether I could read the signs, but I started getting a little concerned. Trying to remain calm, I started banging on the door.

Still no response.

Reality started setting into my five-year-old mind. I can still vividly recall the feelings of confusion, then concern, followed by fear, and finally, sheer terror.

My family had packed up and left me!

I began to cry, starting with a low whimper, and rapidly progressing to screaming at the top of my lungs. Each time I re-read this memory I relive this experience. Our family's babysitter who lived in the home across the street appeared and scooped me up and carried me, by now completely hysterical, to her house.

I don't recall anything else that happened, including when I was reunited with my family. I like to think I blacked out everything else. In truth, I wish I could have blacked out this memory, as it would undoubtedly shape my deep need for security my entire life.

Both of my parents were at work. My older siblings attended a full day of school. I can't recall whether my baby brother had been born. I just remember that I was the first to discover that we had been locked out. It would be years before I would learn that my family had been evicted from our home, which we were renting from a relative. We'd been evicted because my dad didn't pay the rent. I'm certain he never thought a family member would put us out.

The eviction was carried out with such heartlessness, which as an adult I've come to realize was likely not my relative's intent. I had to believe that to make peace with it. But that early, devastating memory of feeling abandoned by my family had a deep, lasting effect. Though I could not put the pieces together for a long time, I would later come to understand why I would work so hard throughout my life to become, and remain, such a fiercely independent woman.

While I plan to share my story chronologically, I can't begin without first giving some critical information and background about my parents. Truthfully, their stories are a lot more interesting than mine.

My Mom's is the story of a strong, tough woman who left her birth country of Japan, her family, and all that she had known at the tender age of twenty-three, to come to America. Born on a poor island in the city of Yokohama Japan, my mother was the last of nine children, born when her mother was forty-two years old, and her father, fifty-two. In provincial Japan in 1935, her parents were considered very old when she was conceived. Heck, in nearly any country, giving birth at forty-two and fathering a child at fifty-two would be considered kind of old.

Mom had four older brothers and four older sisters. She described her family as close, though very poor, living in a small rural town. As the baby of the family, I can only imagine how she was coddled by her older siblings. They all adored this "surprise" baby and aided in her care. Since they were all so much older, they all eventually moved out of the house, leaving Mom alone with her two parents for a few years.

Yokohama was the first harbor city introduced to the world as the entrance to Japan. One of Mom's earliest memories was the Great Yokohama Air Raid during World War II, an attack by the US. Mom was ten years old. This devastating event in which US B-52s dropped firebombs on Yokohama, resulted in the loss of thousands of lives. Throughout her life, Mom vividly remembered the fear and terror that engulfed her family, prompting them to seek shelter underground for their protection. Thankfully, her family emerged physically unharmed from this event.

At the age of thirteen, Mom experienced another life-altering event when her father passed away at age sixty-five. Having just completed elementary school, Mom was forced to quit school and start working to support her mother. Mom shouldered the responsibility of caring for her fifty-five-year-old mother who suffered from severe arthritis and could not work. Additionally, Mom took on the care of her older brother, who had returned home after being diagnosed with cancer. Despite being married and having a family of his own, Mom said her brother didn't like working for a living. When his wife eventually left him and he then got sick, he had no choice but to return home.

One of Mom's other brothers was involved with the Yakuza, the Japanese Mafia. Mom vividly recalls his most striking feature: a magnificent tattoo covering a good part of his body. He also bore a deep scar running from his eyebrow to his chin, which he considered his "battle scar" resulting from his involvement in his chosen profession. For her brother, it was a symbol of honor. Mom remained close to her other siblings and was committed to caring for her family.

When I reflect on how Mom and Dad crossed paths, I am reminded of the scene from the movie "Pretty Woman," where local girls from small towns would doll themselves up on Friday nights and head to the club on the military base. In a similar vein, my mother's older sister, Sumie, invited her to one such gathering. At the time, Sumie was involved with and living with an African American Air Force GI whom she had met at a military base party.

Not intending to brag, but my mom was a gorgeous, sexy woman. She was also very young, naive, and sheltered. Up to that point in her life, she had never ventured beyond her small town of Yokohama. My dad, John was an energetic and bright young man, born and raised in West Philadelphia. Unlike Mom, he was raised by very young parents. His mother got pregnant with him at the age of sixteen, and she and my grandfather were forced to marry.

Following his graduation at age eighteen from Central High School in Philadelphia, Dad enlisted in the Air Force. He had already fathered one child during his teenage years. I don't believe that he and his immediate family ventured out much past Philly and North Carolina, where his parents were from. Hence, his military service introduced this inquisitive, charismatic, and inexperienced young man to an entirely new world. Daddy's first and only overseas Air Force assignment was in Japan.

To understand the limited diversity of the United States during that era, it is essential to note that in 1953, there were very few Japanese people living in the US, and even fewer living on the East Coast of the US. During the 1950's, most Japanese residents in the US were concentrated in Hawaii, California, and along the West Coast. Therefore, it must have been a significant cultural shock for Dad and his fellow American soldiers stationed in Nagano, Japan, to encounter this new "species" of women.

In a manner reminiscent of Pretty Woman, my mother initially viewed this handsome, charismatic American man as her ticket out of poverty. She was not alone in her pursuit. Mom's account of the story was that Dad had fallen in love with her at first sight. And why wouldn't he?

After Mom brought Dad home to introduce him to her family, her brother (the one in the Yakuza) got angry with her and beat her. When she conveyed this story to me, I assumed my uncle had a problem with Dad's race. Of course, the Black side of me was ready to react negatively to having racist family members. But she quickly clarified that the real issue was that her brother did not want her to become involved with an American. To likely a lesser degree than my African ancestors' experience, the first large wave of Japanese immigrants to the US were harshly treated. Her family had also experienced the US's attack on their city where seven to eight thousand Japanese people were killed, and countless others wounded just ten years earlier.

After this incident with her brother, Mom packed her things and moved into her sister Sumie's house. Mom fell in love with Dad, and they had a whirlwind courtship. Within months after they met, Dad proposed marriage to Mom. She immediately said yes. Both were about to turn twenty-one, Mom in January and Dad in February. Since he was only twenty years old at the time, Dad needed his parents' permission to get married. He wrote them to let them know he'd met the woman he wanted to marry. Would they provide their permission? Probably more out of sheer ignorance, they wrote him back and both refused to give them their consent. In the true fashion of the determined man who, in my years growing up was never known to take no for an answer, Dad was undeterred. He turned twenty-one on February 19th, 1956, and promptly married Mom the next day, on February 20th.

Shortly after, Mom moved to the Air Force base, and the newlyweds settled into married life. Mom became pregnant almost immediately, and just ten months after they married, the young family joyfully welcomed my older sister. Mom's family celebrated the birth of this beautiful baby with great joy.

For the most part, it was a joyous time. However, Mom faced challenges adjusting to life away from her family for the first time. Despite regular visits from her family members, Mom began to experience homesickness. It wasn't long before she realized that her new husband was likely not ready for the responsibility he now assumed. But by then, they were married and had a child together. Those early months of marriage were tough on Mom, and she found herself falling into depression. Although she didn't label it as such back then, she knew she frequently experienced sadness. When I asked her how she got through it, she told me she just learned to "suck it up."

If Mom was lamenting the major changes in her life up to that point, life was about to become even more interesting. After Dad completed his assignment in Japan, they were transferred to Montana. Mom and Dad began preparing to return to Dad's home country, the United States, with his new wife and daughter. This devastated my maternal grandmother, as she loved her baby granddaughter with all her heart, and begged Mom to leave her in

Japan with her family. My sister was a beautiful blend of her African American father's curly hair and darker brown skin, and her Japanese mother's bone-straight hair and fair skin. Though her skin was fair, it was a tad darker than full-blooded Japanese babies and she stood out. Like in many other cultures, colorism existed in that rural, provincial town of Yokohama.

Throughout Japanese culture, lighter skin was, and continues to be, valued more than darker skin. A backlash began brewing around American servicemen coming to Japan and dating Japanese women, in many cases abandoning women they impregnated. There are many stories of servicemen approaching their superiors expressing an interest in marrying a Japanese woman, and then being immediately shipped out and reassigned to another country, or back to the US. It was especially frowned upon when those servicemen were Black. Many of the racially mixed children, "hafu" or half-Japanese and half non-Japanese, ended up abandoned or sent to orphanages, doomed to live with the stigma of being unwanted, and unwelcome in their own country of birth.

Because of the prejudice that existed among many Japanese people, my mother was afraid to leave my sister in Japan. The truth was, she also couldn't imagine parting with her first-born child. I totally get it. I know I would not have been able to do that.

Having never ventured beyond her small hometown of Yokohama, Mom was saddened to leave her family. At the same time, she was indescribably excited. She was going to America with her new husband and beloved baby girl, where she believed all her dreams would come true.

Before Dad reported for duty at his new US assignment, he took his new wife and daughter to meet his parents in Philadelphia, PA. What awaited her was not exactly what she had envisioned when she married what seemed to be a wealthy American military man whom she followed to another country.

Daddy had married this foreign woman, exposing her to a whole new world, and he now informed her that he expected her to assimilate and blend in. I can't even begin to imagine how Mom must have felt. I can't blame Dad. He was a twenty-three-year-old unworldly young man who had no sense of the magnitude of his request.

Once on US soil, Daddy then told Mom that they would no longer speak Japanese, even though he spoke the language fluently. I can't fathom the courage Mom had to summon. At the tender age of twenty-three, she packed up and moved away from her family, her culture, and all that she knew to go to another country. She had limited knowledge of the English language and was unfamiliar with the culture, the customs, and pretty much anything else American. On top of all that, Mom faced outright racism in the US from the beginning, as many Americans held negative views of military brides, particularly those from Far East countries. The media fueled this sentiment, alleging that the Japanese, especially Japanese women, took advantage of and exploited American servicemen for personal gain.

It wasn't until much later in my life when I fully understood the racial climate in both Japan and the US, did I realize the true courage Daddy displayed in marrying Mom and bringing her to this country.

Unlike Mom's parents who were long married and much older when Mom was born, Dad's parents were teenagers when he was born. Although not uncommon at that time, Dad was raised by parents who were just kids themselves, forced to take on adult responsibilities.

Not afforded the option or luxury of attending college, both of his parents got respectable jobs at the Post Office, lived a comfortable middle-class life, and did their best to build a life together. My grandparents had two more sons together, and eventually divorced. They both eventually remarried.

Because of his own scars, Daddy didn't know what to do with this young wife whom he brought to another country, who couldn't speak the language at all. Mom would soon learn that Daddy meant it when he said that they would no longer speak Japanese. Mom had to learn English, and quickly. Sounds tough right? It was. Back then, other countries were not focused on teaching English as a second language as so many are today. Assimilating into American culture was commonplace among families of all different ethnicities emigrating to the US.

My parents' top priority in coming to the US was for Mom to meet her in-laws. From the beginning, Mom sensed that her mother-in-law didn't like her. After all, neither she nor my grandfather had given my dad permission to marry this woman. He had disobeyed them, and Mom felt that my grandmother blamed my mother.

Fortunately, my father's grandmother, Nana, adored and cherished my mother and sister from the moment she met them. Mom and Nana developed a close relationship that would last until Nana passed away many years later.

After a short visit, Dad moved the family to Montana to report for his new assignment. They both settled back into military life and for Mom, the reality of all that she'd left behind set in. She was deeply homesick, navigating in a foreign world. Because she could not read nor write in English, she felt lost and experienced a deep sense of loneliness and not belonging. She knew there was no option to return to Japan. Mom determined that she would do what she needed to do for her family in the US.

Mom recalls a funny story about how she decided to surprise my father and went grocery shopping. When she returned home, she was quite proud of herself. The moment Dad returned from work that evening, Mom showed him her purchases. Much to her dismay, Dad started laughing. Mom had been shopping in the pet aisle and brought home dried cat food and canned dog food! I can only conclude that they must not have had pictures on the labels. Mom thought the dry cat food was cereal. As I think back on it now, I chuckle, and hope my sister wasn't fed cat food!

A few months later, Mom discovered she was pregnant again, and my parents welcomed a second daughter, Beatrice. However, shortly thereafter, tragedy struck the young family. At only two months of age, Beatrice died from sudden infant death syndrome (SIDS), commonly known as crib death. Mom took the loss of her daughter extremely hard. She fell into a depression, struggling to care for her first-born daughter and be a good wife.

Dad was often away, leaving Mom alone to deal with her daughter and her grief. She had no friends in Montana. Mom relayed to me that this was one of the hardest periods of her life up to that point. Fortunately, within months the young family was transferred to Santa Barbara, California.

A few months after settling there, Mom discovered she was once again pregnant, and she was overjoyed. Just over a year after the loss of her second daughter, Mom gave birth to my brother, John Jr. Fearing she might lose Johnny as well, she became overly protective, never letting him out of her sight. She checked his breathing every few hours and barely slept. Despite the anxiety, she said she was happy.

When Johnny was three months old, Mom found out she was pregnant again, with me. Initially, she and Daddy decided to put me up for adoption. I don't know what changed their minds, nor why Mom shared this information with me many years later. I sometimes wonder what would have become of me if I had been adopted, but I am confident that I am right where I need to be.

I joked with Mom that she got pregnant a lot. She confessed that no one had ever explained birth control to her. Based on that, I suppose she was lucky not to have gotten pregnant even more frequently.

After I was born, it would be another five years before my baby brother Steven came along. By that point, Mom was thousands of miles away from her own family, with three children, no marketable skills, a young husband, and a challenging relationship with her mother-in-law. My mother faced some tough challenges.

After Mom moved to the US, Mom's sister Sumie continued to support Mom as her best friend and confidante. By then, Sumie had started practicing Buddhism in Japan. Mom would call Sumie and pour out her loneliness, constantly crying on her shoulder. Sumie always listened, cried with her, and consistently encouraged Mom to try practicing Buddhism to change her situation.

There are countless studies and stories about immigrants of all ethnicities who suffer mental, social, psychological and physical challenges after migrating. Mom was certainly not alone. Every aspect of an immigrant's life changes, deeply affecting their world views, concepts of self, cultural and social support systems, and everything in between.

Mom repeatedly declined her sister's encouragement to try

Buddhism until she said she began to experience a feeling of hopelessness. When she reached what she referred to as her lowest point, Mom finally agreed to try Buddhism. I was three years old at the time.

Once she embraced Buddhism, Mom began to immediately feel more hopeful and experience positive changes in her life. She fully embraced the practice. Sumie reached out all the way from Japan to the Buddhist organization in Philadelphia to connect Mom with the members. This organization was built by many Japanese military brides in the 1960s. It's the same sect of Buddhism that the late Tina Turner practiced. Practicing Buddhism changed my mother's life in so many ways, which had far-reaching positive effects on her family. I can say that it had a powerful impact on my siblings and me as children. Mom introduced hundreds of people to Buddhism and found happiness and peace in her life, despite ongoing challenges for her and Dad.

Finding Our Cultural Connections and Community

Thankfully, one of the many benefits of our amazing Buddhist community was the unconditional acceptance we received. It was also in that community that we saw and interacted with others who looked like us. It was a safe place for us. How could we not have been attracted to this religion and practice? Mom developed life-long relationships with many of the Japanese members she met. They spoke her language, shared similar experiences adjusting to US culture, and comforted one another through their feelings of homesickness.

Of the many benefits of connecting to our Japanese heritage was the food! Those Japanese women could cook, and all the members of all races and ethnicities, ages and genders alike loved the food. I have so many fond memories of long bus trips we'd take to attend large Buddhist meetings in other cities and states, and the Japanese women would pull out those yummy rice balls, fish cakes, and perfectly seasoned Japanese vegetables!

Attending the Buddhist meetings and hearing others share their experiences truly encouraged me. When I was a child, I prayed (chanted) to get what I wanted. When I experienced problems, I chanted and always got results. Later in life, I became more consistent, and my practice expanded from being self-focused to helping, praying for, and encouraging others. Buddhism remains for me now a daily practice.

Dad came from a family of long-standing Baptists, so as children we were exposed to both religions at young ages. At one point after seeing the improvement in Mom's life, Dad started practicing Buddhism. That didn't last that long, but once Mom embraced Buddhism, she committed to a life-long practice.

Seeing my mother's life-long success despite the countless odds against her that most of us never had to encounter, each of her children made the conscious decision to continue practicing throughout our adult lives.

My mother was the one constant in my life until I went away to college. Mom was my greatest source of inspiration, motivation, and support, and was truly my (s)hero in every sense of the word.

Mom was also my harshest critic, and our relationship has always been complex. Neither I nor my siblings would ever get to meet our maternal grandmother, so I never got to experience my mother's dynamics with her mother. The last time Mom saw her mother was in 1958, when she, Daddy, and my sister left Japan. Many years later, we would learn that my maternal grandmother died from a terrible fall in the late 1980s.

Over the next decades as our family's collective circumstances improved, Mom did get to make several trips to Japan to spend long periods with her family, and she also went on Buddhist pilgrimages.

My relationship with my mother and her incredible influence on me is a hard subject for me to tackle. In American culture and most others, it is considered taboo to speak of our mothers in anything other than a positive light. Mothers are deservedly elevated and revered in our society, as they often serve as the backbones of our families, regardless of culture. My mother was undoubtedly our family's backbone.

This cultural judgment against anyone expressing anything other than praise for their mothers can be harsh. It is one of the reasons why many daughters and sons with complicated relationships with their mothers remain silent and never address or seek the help we might need.

Consequently, we carry our emotional wounds with us, hidden in both invisible and visible baggage that influences our perception of the world and shapes our journey through life. This experience of normalizing our upbringing and assuming it to be the norm is not exclusive to Japanese culture, although it is often joked about among my Asian friends. Our tough moms, and the fear we have of them – these sentiments resonate with my Black friends and friends who are children of immigrants as well. Unfortunately, the silence we endure due to the taboo around discussing these matters only adds to our suffering.

My challenges with her don't take away from the fact that my mother was also incredibly giving, self-sacrificing and inspiring to so many. Nearly everyone who has encountered her has at least one great story to share. She was bigger than life, amazing, wonderful, and human. The way I see life and how I've navigated this journey is largely influenced by my relationship with her. I am deeply grateful that the universe graced me with her as my mother.

I've also had many other mother-like figures in my life. I have been incredibly fortunate to have experienced profound maternal love and acceptance from not just my mom, but also my paternal grandmother, my late and current mothers-in-law, my best childhood friend's mother, my current best friend's mother, and many others, who have all played a significant role in my life.

Some of the Japanese women in our Buddhist organization

served as mother figures as well. Just as with Black Moms, Japanese moms didn't only mother their own children. Connecting to the Buddhist organization that consisted of and many Japanese military brides enabled us to embrace and learn more about our Japanese culture in so many other respects.

I'm now taking you back to that fateful day when I came home to the padlocked doors. After being evicted, our family lived temporarily with my paternal grandmother, and then with my father's best friend and his wife. I recall longing for a home for just me and my family. My wish would soon become a reality.

When I was in either first or second grade, we moved into our very own three-bedroom apartment in a development with a fancy name. You'll find this hard to believe, but it wasn't until decades later that I would learn that we lived in the "projects," short for Public Housing Project. Projects are government-owned housing for low-income residents.

I loved our new home. My brothers shared one bedroom, my sister and I shared another, and my parents occupied the third. I was happy we finally had our own space.

There's a Japanese proverb: "I no naka no kawazu taikai wo shirazu," which translates to "The frog in a well knows nothing of the sea." This saying encapsulates the fact that our perspectives are often limited by our own experiences.

Most of this development's residents were Black. I think I recall a few white families as well. There were no Japanese or any other Asians around, and people weren't familiar with Japanese people in general. Due to the prevalence of Chinese products and the representation of Chinese people on TV, many Americans referred to all Asians as Chinese.

Understandably, the level of ignorance regarding people

who are different from the majority is sort of expected. It's an understatement to say that people didn't know what to think of us. The racial climate in America in many areas was anti-Asian, or rather, anti-anyone or anything perceived as different. There was an ongoing debate as well as significant backlash against "Afro-Asian" babies in both Japan and the US that lasted for over a decade.

This ignorance and intolerance for those who were different would define a good part of the first couple of decades of my life. Little did I know how much my childhood, adolescence, and early adulthood would be marked by recurring episodes of teasing, harassment, and discrimination within my neighborhoods and schools.

I've realized over time that much of the mistreatment I encountered from others stemmed from a genuine curiosity borne out of a lack of exposure to and understanding of individuals who were neither white nor black. I hear people my age lament that the bullying of young people today is out of control, and it wasn't like that when we were young. I don't know what world you grew up in! Trust me, I have the receipts.

A by-product of my encounters with bullies was that at a young age, I developed a stoic demeanor and what appeared to many to be a hardened exterior. I didn't see it as a "hardness," but rather a "calm under pressure." This "calm," once I learned to harness it effectively, has evolved into a resilience that has stayed with me and served me well throughout my life.

I think my fascination with swans at a young age influenced my development of this stoic demeanor. I can't recall where, but I remember my reaction the first time I saw a group of swans in a pond. They were so graceful and elegant. I had no clue how much their webbed feet were working under the surface to give the appearance of their calm above the surface. I began to read about swans and deepened my knowledge about them. My spirit animal today is the swan.

Fitting in at Home, School and Among Family

While the resentment of my Japanese mom was obvious among many neighbors, some embraced my mother and treated us like family. Aunt Emma, a strong black mother of three, took Mom under her wing and taught her so much. She introduced Mom to someone who could do something with our biracial grades of hair, gave us the "ins and outs" around whom to associate and whom to avoid, helped Mom with her cooking, and provided us with love and support. My brother Steven said she taught Mom how to say the "N" word, which was not as politically incorrect at that time! Her children were our "cousins" with whom we played. They provided us with protection in our neighborhood when possible.

It was the middle of the school year when I transferred to a new elementary school. By that time, all student friendships and alliances had been set. They had morning and afternoon restroom breaks. On my first day there, the teacher instructed us to line up in pairs to go to the restroom together. I looked around at everyone and went to one girl and proclaimed to her that she would be my bathroom partner. She told me that she already had a bathroom partner. The way she said it made me so mad that I punched her in her back!

What the heck?

I was shocked at my reaction. Where did that come from? I immediately came to regret it when I learned that the person I punched came from a big family, and many of her siblings and cousins attended this school. I got in trouble with the teacher, but that was a minor consequence in comparison to the reactions I got from my fellow students. The girl I hit whispered in my ear that she was going to beat me up at the end of the day.

Man, I had gotten off to a rough start. Throughout that day, students came by and looked in the window of the classroom. Many pointed at me and smirked. Word of what this new kid had done rapidly spread throughout the school, and I was honestly terrified for what was to come. The day dragged on forever, with my anxiety growing by the minute.

The dreaded end of the day finally came. We all exited into the schoolyard, where it seemed like the entire student body was waiting. The students surrounded us. I couldn't run if I wanted to. They were all instigating, and her family members were yelling at her to hit me. I was terrified, but stood my ground, determined to not show how afraid I was!

For some reason that is still unknown to me, she never hit me. All I can surmise is that she must have thought if this little skinny, funny-looking girl dared to hit her, she may not have known what to expect. Or maybe she felt sorry for me.

But we never fought. I know she took major flack for it. The funny thing was, we eventually ended up being friends.

My siblings and I had so many experiences in that neighborhood. My older sister, my brother, and I were constantly teased and bullied. The simple truth was we just never fit in.

Meanwhile, I believe our young parents did the best they could to create a life for us. Although my dad was not the most responsible adult, he made consistent efforts to embrace his roles as a husband, father, and responsible individual. He was very intelligent and always managed to secure well-paying jobs. For one reason or another, he would eventually quit or lose them. During my childhood, our family frequently moved, forcing us to start over and repeatedly go through the process of fitting in. As I looked back, each of these moves helped us to further develop our resilience, making it easier to adapt to any environment in which we found ourselves.

Shortly after we moved into our apartment, my mom secured a job at a bible publishing company that paid her enough to cover rent, utilities, and the family's essential needs. We had very little money for extras, but she made every penny stretch as far as possible. She remained with that company, binding bibles until she retired in her early sixties.

My parents' coming of age occurred in a different era, before the advent of social media, during a time when it was not uncommon for men and women to engage in multiple relationships. I had numerous friends whose fathers had multiple families and different sets of children. Later in life, I would meet my dad's first son, who was born around the same time Dad entered the military.

When I got my own DNA results, I discovered that I probably have another older brother as well. In Dad's defense, both the first and the suspected second brother I found were born before he met my mother.

My parents would struggle with this aspect as Mom would never be comfortable with Dad's *entanglements*. Mom and Dad had a relationship filled with peaks and valleys. When things, were good, they were great. When things got ugly, they got really ugly. Dad was very much a hands-off husband and father who as my mom put it, frequently "ran the streets." I wish I could recall more memories with him during my formative years, but I simply cannot.

By most accounts, I was considered a "Good Daughter." I don't say this with pride, as it came at a price. At least one of my siblings still feels that my dad treated me differently. To some extent, that was true. If you believed in the philosophy that "children should be seen and not heard," then I was the epitome of that. I was painfully shy (although no one who knows me now would believe it), possessed a significant fear of authority, and constantly sought to please others. My siblings labeled me a "goody two shoes," which hurt me, even though I never let on that it bothered me.

Instead, I responded by doubling down on good behavior, as it resulted in positive reinforcement from the adults in my life. This pattern of seeking approval through good behavior and achievement would become a recurring theme throughout my life. I have to say I was also a "tattletale," which wasn't a good thing, and I knew it. If you aren't familiar with that term, the modern-day word for it is "snitch." I definitely brought some punishment on myself.

I made some major mistakes and missteps over the years. None were due to intellectual deficiencies, but rather, bad judgment. While in the third or fourth grade, I made my first life-altering mistake in my quest to fit in. Because of my deep need to be liked, I began "acting" like I wasn't smart around my friends. I differentiate "acting" from "dumbing myself down" because I worked hard in my classes. At a very young age, I learned how to "code-switch," or present different versions of myself based on the situation. I had no idea that was what I was doing. I just wanted to fit in. That was a common phenomenon that even thirty-plus years later, my children were accused of.

How little do we think of ourselves and our ethnicity that when we hear someone speaking proper English, we associate it with "talking white?" Even my closest friend at the time (or should I say "frenemy" because she came from a big family of bullies), and others teased me about being smart. She, like many of my fellow students, did not take either education or earning good grades as seriously as my Asian mother. Good grades were extremely important to Mom, as in their culture, good grades and achievement are reflections on them as parents.

My teacher was going to recommend me for admission into a well-known school for gifted children in Philadelphia. The school notified my parents. Admission was based on grades and standardized test scores.

Peer pressure dictated my next move. As we had done every year, all the students at my elementary school took the California Achievement test. I was about halfway through the test when my frenemy "Mandy" appeared at the window of my classroom and motioned for me to join her. Back then, when you completed your test, you could begin your recess. Eager to join my friend, I started randomly filling in the circles of the multiple-choice answers without even looking at the questions. Unsurprisingly, my test results were uncharacteristically poor. My parents, and Mom in particular, were shocked.

As a parent, I look back on that and wonder why no one ever questioned the marked difference in the scores that year versus an established pattern of high scores in previous years. Had that occurred with my children, I know I would have seen that break in pattern as a red flag, and immediately questioned it.

My teacher, Mr. Stevens, saw what my parents did not question. He knew I was smart, and he questioned me on the poor test scores. However, he couldn't do anything with his concerns without a parent actively advocating for me. Looking back, I don't blame my mother. She had no formal schooling and was still learning how to read and write English herself. I don't' recall Dad helping me with schoolwork or homework. He always praised me and told me how smart I was. Looking back, I suspect he may have thought I didn't need his help.

My childhood realization that I could not always rely on my parents, likely accounts for why I sometimes over-analyzed or over-thought situations, and why I would (and still) fiercely advocate for my children. This tendency would later serve me well, but also create greater challenges at different points in my life.

I'd been forced to learn to advocate for myself at a young age. It would be years before I could pinpoint the sources of this need for this level of self-reliance, and begin to understand, accept and re-channel that energy to work it to my advantage.

As a result of my California Achievement Test debacle, there was no further discussion of my transferring schools. As a fifth grader, I was put into the same class as my one-year-older brother and the rest of the sixth graders. And because of those test scores, I was in sixth grade again the following year. That was my first life-altering decision based on bad judgment due to my need to belong. Unfortunately, it wouldn't be my last. Not only did my siblings and I worry about acclimating and fitting in at school, but at times we also had to figure it out within our middle-class Black family. Because we looked differently than everyone else, we didn't always feel like we fit in. I also sensed that some family members looked down on my mom. While I'm confident that our relatives had good intentions, their actions were sometimes challenging to understand.

One summer some relatives took me and my older brother Johnny to the "country" where they owned a vacation home. As soon as we arrived, our relatives took us shopping for new clothing. I loved it all, as well as the luxury of wearing a new outfit every day. I recall that the clothing was more "girly" (and I'm certain better quality) than the clothing I was accustomed to wearing, but I was grateful to have received new clothing!

My brother and I immensely enjoyed that summer trip. We ran around and played, caught lightning bugs, climbed a plum tree that grew over a pig pen, and ate as many plums as we wanted.

We didn't see the clothing Mom packed for us until the end of the week, on the day we were leaving. I loved my new clothing and was excited that I'd be able to wear my new stuff when I returned home. Our relatives told us the clothing would remain at the house and promised us that we would be able to again wear it the following year when we returned. We wore our old clothing home.

When we got home, I told my mom that we got new clothing that we could wear when we went back next summer. Her response was less enthusiastic than mine. It wasn't until I was older that I pieced together what happened and understood my mother's reaction.

The clothes were meant to make us look a certain way while we were there, a temporary investment in our appearance. It would have been more generous to let us take the clothes home with us. Instead, they became an expensive investment for just one week of wear. The way young children grow, it was unlikely that we would have been able to fit them the following year. This was another situation where, as an adult I realized that our relatives' intentions were probably good. They were decent and loving people. They just had no sense of how their actions would be received by others. I don't recall if my brother and I ever returned to that vacation home.

In other instances, I witnessed my mother being treated differently and our poor family being looked down upon by relatives.

For some reason, I always held an unwavering confidence at my humble beginnings were temporary. I always had an unshakable belief within me that I possessed the determination and ability to mold my own existence. My commitment to my daily Buddhist practice was also a cornerstone in my life, continuously propelling my personal growth across every dimension. I was convinced that my potential knew no bounds. And I lived my life with that conviction.

"Living well is the best revenge."
- The late Helen Gurley Brown,
former editor of Cosmopolitan Magazine

That quote became an instant and consistent inspiration for me to create a meaningful life for myself.

I have to say that overall, I had a happy childhood. I spent most of my early days hanging with my brother and his friends. I loved hanging out with boys because at that age, there was little drama, and the activities the boys engaged in were more fun to me than the stuff the girls did. But what brother wants his kid sister hanging around him and his friends?

I spent entire dodgeball games dodging balls my brother lodged at me. I grew to understand the why as I got older. But back then, it was easier to get picked on by him than by the mean girls. I was not afraid of the boys and much more comfortable around them.

My brother made it a point to make me the target of whatever game we were playing, and he and I fought constantly. I was born a day before his first birthday, and I jokingly say it took him a long time to forgive me for ruining his first birthday party!

I recall us getting into physical fights at school and the two of us were the only ones in detention. There was one of many fights when we were both at home alone. One such fight felt like it lasted for hours. After we were both completely exhausted, we went into our respective rooms. I'd pulled his hair enough to bust a blood vessel in his head. He chipped one of my two front teeth. My parents never took him to a hospital, nor me to the dentist, so it would not be until the summer after my freshman year of college that I would get my tooth fixed.

As I look back, I almost believe that my parents intentionally left my tooth cracked, as my unique look caught the eyes of many boys. My Dad hated it when boys looked at me. But the reality is that my parents never took us to doctors or dentists unless we were really sick or injured. As many poor people still consider it as such today, the ER was our doctor's office.

As much as my brother and I fought as kids, he and I became very close as adults. He is one of the warmest, kindest men you'll ever meet.

It was also around this time that I began to develop my love for fashion. Despite being labeled a "tomboy" back then and having limited clothing options, I was inspired by my second-grade teacher, Miss Chapman. She was a beautiful, statuesque Black woman who walked into our classroom like she was rolling into a fashion show every day. She was also classy and caring. It was not just her fashion sense, but it was the way she carried herself, so poised and confident.

She was knowledgeable, well-traveled, and most importantly, very interesting. I decided that I wanted to be just like Miss Chapman when I grew up. I wasn't sure how I'd get there, but one thing I developed at a young age was resourcefulness. This resourcefulness became one of my defining traits from a young age, and I had no qualms about accepting free help, things, experiences, training, or exposure.

Unlike many people in my neighborhood, I gladly welcomed and accepted everything offered to me. When volunteers came to work with us "disadvantaged children" in our neighborhood, I made sure I was there. I learned how to make crafts, received free swimming lessons, learned to cook and crochet from my paternal grandmother, attended charm school in junior high, learned to garden in my teens, learned to tap dance, and so much more.

Like most Asian children, I also played musical instruments. In elementary school, I played the violin, and as one of the first Buddhist Junior Pioneers in Philadelphia, I played the piccolo. I excelled at spelling and won my elementary school's Spelling Bee championship when I was in fifth grade. I went on to compete in the city-wide championship sponsored by the Bulletin Newspaper, where I came in second place for the entire city of Philadelphia. I lost to an eleventh grader from West Philadelphia High School. I still remember the word I misspelled:

EXORBITANT.

I had added an unnecessary "H." Despite my achievement, my parents and I left the Spelling Bee feeling disappointed. It didn't matter that I had won second place as a fifth grader competing against high schoolers. I learned that success was measured in an "all or nothing" manner. As a reward for my placement in the competition, I, along with the spelling champion, appeared on the Joel Spivak TV show. I also received a Merriam-Webster dictionary that I cherished. The dictionary was a pretty cool prize! I think I lost it during one of my moves after the birth of my sons.

Fortunately, I evolved into a person who believes in celebrating victories, even if isn't always the grand prize. I'm also grateful that I didn't instill that mindset of absolute "all or nothing" in my children. Conversely, I don't buy into the "everyone deserves a trophy" mindset either. Though I strove for ultimate victory and encouraged my sons and those who worked on any of my teams to do so, it was never perfection I was seeking. Well, most of the time it wasn't. I was, and still can be a bit of a perfectionist.

Some parts of my life weren't so pleasant. There was a boy, Harry Mack, who annoyed and teased the hell out of me for years. He chased me home from school nearly daily for at least a year. Initially, I complained about him to my family and my school. During those days, the school didn't get involved in what would

31

now be characterized as harassment. To them, it was just a silly boy with a crush. I complained to my dad. One day, Dad was home in the middle of the day, waiting for Harry. As soon as he saw him, Dad chased him. I went into our apartment and lost sight of them. After a while, Dad came home but never mentioned what happened. Neither did Harry, though unfortunately, my father's presence didn't faze him. He resumed chasing me home that same week.

During that fifth-grade year, I befriended the most popular, prettiest, and best-dressed girl, Sharon Jordan. I liked her so much I'd walk ten minutes further away from the school (and my apartment) and wait for her so we could walk to school together. I was overjoyed that a girl like her wanted to be friends with me. We became good friends. I became part of the "cool kids." That is, until she learned that the boy she liked, liked me. Stupid Harry Mack. I had zero interest in boys, and I hated him. I went out of my way to convince her that I didn't like him. But I could feel when the shift started occurring in our friendship. She began keeping me at arm's length and slowly pulling away.

Sharon befriended another classmate, Wendy, who was also thrilled to be her friend. To this day, I'm not sure what the final trigger was, but I fell out of favor with Sharon, and she grew closer to Wendy. Sharon instigated a fight between Wendy and me. I was a painfully skinny little girl, but I didn't back down from anyone, even then. Wendy was twice my size, and only too happy to fight me to solidify the approval of the pretty popular girl, my former friend. This was the one fight I knew I would lose, and I did. Wendy beat me up.

After that incident, I was ostracized. But don't start feeling sorry for me. I started spending time alone, and surprisingly, enjoyed it. I could sleep a little later since I no longer got up earlier to go to Sharon's house in the morning. I could embrace my intelligence and be comfortable with it. I also spent less time thinking about what to wear, since I considered myself to now be invisible to others. The alternative was not bad at all.

As far back as I can recall, I loved reading and began immersing myself even more in books. I embraced the whole "outsider" persona. My confidence grew, and I learned to enjoy my own company.

Shortly thereafter, an Asian girl moved into an adjacent neighborhood. Unlike me, Susan was fully Asian. Both of her parents were Chinese. But Susan looked more like me than any of the other students. Like me, she was smart, committed to getting good grades, played a musical instrument, and loved reading.

Consistent with the treatment I received when I came to the school, the other students kept their distance from her. Everyone except me. Susan and I became fast friends. Everyone else largely ignored us or appeared to. I recall a school trip where Susan and I created our own unique language by using initials creatively. We used the language to communicate with one another on the bus, leaving our classmates puzzled and trying to decode our secret language. Call us petty, but Susan and I delighted in the fact that they never figured it out. Susan was super-smart. I loved that I had a friend who was proud of her intelligence. It made me more comfortable with embracing my own.

At our sixth-grade graduation, Susan was the valedictorian, and I was the salutatorian. Unfortunately, after graduation, I never saw Susan again.

During my elementary school years, Mom and Dad had undergone numerous separations and reconciliations. During sixth grade, while Mom and Dad were separated, Dad began a new relationship and moved into his girlfriend's house. My brothers and I sometimes visited him, and we all liked his new girlfriend. That summer, Mom made one of the toughest decisions of her life. She decided that Dad should take responsibility for me and my siblings and told him to take us to live with him. Mom wanted to move out of the apartment and closer to her job. So, a few weeks after elementary school graduation, my brothers and I moved to West Philadelphia and into Dad's girlfriend's home. Miss Regina had no children but kindly agreed to help care for the three of us. Looking back, that was a lot to ask of a childless woman in a relatively new relationship.

Excited and delighted were both understatements. I was leaving a house with very strict rules laid down by Mom. She lived by the code that her kids be inside by the time the streetlights came on. Our bedtime at Mom's was 8:30 pm during the school year and 10 pm during the summer. I had very little latitude as far as venturing outside of my neighborhood.

Initially, moving to Miss Regina's place brought me happiness. I enjoyed my newfound freedom. My siblings and I could sleep late and stay outside as late as we wanted. She cooked every day, and we could eat whenever we wanted. It felt like a vacation since we didn't have school during the summer, and I don't recall having any chores. Daddy was completely hands-off. It was Heaven.

My siblings and I made new friends. Of course, the anxiety around looking different and figuring out how to fit in also kicked in. We were the new Chinese kids in the neighborhood. The teasing was a given. It was also another time when I faced intense peer pressure. I followed the crowd of neighborhood kids my age and started smoking cigarettes. I remember the initial puff—it was terrible. It made me dizzy and caused me to cough. Despite not enjoying smoking, I persisted because I thought it made me look cool and helped me to fit in. I smoked cigarettes for several years during my teen years. Fortunately, once I saw pictures of blackened lungs in a science class, I quit cold turkey.

I was settling into a new home and environment and adjusting to major life changes. That fall, I entered a new junior high school and felt like I had a fresh beginning. The usual anxiety around having to acclimate, make new friends, and figure out ways to fit in was magnified since I had to do the same at my new school. Unbeknownst to me then, this was a significant turning point in my life.

It was one of my most challenging periods up to that point, and I was learning a lot about myself. The recurring theme of the funny-looking Black Japanese girl once again surfaced. I would venture to say that I was the only Black Japanese student in the school, at least that I knew of. There was the expected bullying. But by this time, I had honed my interpersonal skills and was becoming an experienced people pleaser. At the same time, I had developed a bit of feistiness. I sometimes put on that tough facade, making myself unpredictable to others. I was also beginning to learn the value of possessing a self-deprecating sense of humor, using it when necessary to disarm people. I embraced the various facets of my personality and learned to adjust my behavior to navigate different situations.

Looking back, I realize I was honing my social survival skills. On top of it all, I was transforming from a little girl into a young woman, and with that came all the hormone shifting that accompanies that evolution. It was also becoming more challenging to make myself invisible. Fortunately, I found myself experiencing less of a need to do that. As time passed, my distinct Asian features began to soften, and I gained control over my wild, curly hair.

During this time, I also began to discover the power of the combination of my achievements, intelligence, physical beauty, and kindness. This combination, strategically balanced, served me well. However, these four characteristics sometimes made me unpopular among others, including some friends.

Half the time, I had this innocent ignorance about me. Still, I started learning to pick up on signs and to figure out how to neutralize the power others seemed to have over me. One incident that stands out showed me just how much I had evolved. It was in seventh grade during a Chemistry class, about a month after I started attending this school. As soon as I entered the classroom, everyone fell silent. The teacher had not yet arrived, but most of the students were already in the classroom. I had that familiar sense that I was the target of a joke. I braced myself, knowing it probably wouldn't be pleasant. I tried to calm my racing heart.

It was that annoying Jim. I recall his full name to this day, and I'd easily recognize him in a line-up. As it turned out, he wrote a song about me. He had been sharing the lyrics before I'd entered the classroom.

I took a deep breath and asked him to sing the song. He looked at me strangely, but he complied. After all, he had an audience. They were clearly entertained by it before I entered the room.

He sang the song. I can still hear it in my mind. It was something about rice paddies — a reference to my Asian ethnicity. It was a couple of verses long, so it was clear that he took some time to compose it. He had also composed a catchy tune to go with it. Believe it or not, I still remember the words and the tune.

Once he finished singing, he and the other students awaited my response. Again, a "never let them see you sweat" moment. I was fuming inside. This was indeed a "swan" moment. Cool on the surface, webbed feet paddling furiously under the water.

I asked myself: "What would he not expect?" I had also been known to curse people out, but that would have been the expected response. Instead, I responded by smiling, thanking him for taking the time to write a song about me and expressed how special I felt. I then turned around to face the front of the class. I'm certain that he and most of the students in the class thought I was too dumb to know I was supposed to be the butt of the joke. I don't recall much else. Deep down, I felt a sense of victory.

I had taken my power back.

I would use that same tactic of confusing people and turning the tables on them many times. It's astonishing how empowering it can be. Reflecting on the incident, I considered Jim's time and energy in thinking about me and coming up with the idea of composing a song to embarrass me. Whether it stemmed from curiosity, an attraction of some sort, or perhaps a fear of someone different, I didn't need to figure out the "why." What I do know is there were no more songs written about me.

Adjusting to other aspects of my new life was great. I got to use my school's pool and recreation facilities, which were new at that time. I improved from being a good swimmer to becoming an excellent swimmer. I think it was during this period that I also began transforming from being what was at the time labeled a "tom boy" to a young lady interested in how I looked. I began to take more interest in my appearance. I attended and truly enjoyed charm school. I recall when I first learned to walk like a young lady. I felt different and more confident. Yes, someone had to show me, and I had to practice! I also had the opportunity to participate in fashion shows and loved it all!

Meanwhile, Mom was settled into her new home. Living alone for the first time in her life, she'd found her new apartment, signed her lease, coordinated with movers and was enjoying her newfound freedom.

I was especially proud of her, as she had just recently brought up the circumstances surrounding my kindergarten experience when I came home to padlocked doors.

She relayed that she initially couldn't grasp what happened when we were evicted from our home. Back in Japan, she and her family lived in one house her entire life. She didn't understand the concept of renting, nor the possibility that someone could remove you from your own home. Those of us in this country take this knowledge for granted. For her, adjusting to life away from the comfort and security of her homeland and her family had to be challenging.

When I went to visit her, I liked her place. I liked this calm version of Mom I experienced in her new surroundings.

Back at my new home with my dad, I continued to experience many positive things as well. No one cared whether I studied. As a result, I rarely studied. As wonderful as Miss Regina was, it wasn't her responsibility to make sure we handled our school commitments. She was a single woman living alone before her home was taken over by this man and his three children. Fortunately, I didn't find the schoolwork to be that hard. This newfound freedom was great for a while.

Yet, this sounds unbelievable even now as I write it, but at twelve years of age, I realized that I needed more structure. I started missing certain things. What I missed most was my mother.

Time To Go Home, B.

I don't recall all the details, but on the following New Year's Day, I packed up my few belongings and took the two buses on public transportation to my mother's new home, a two-bedroom apartment. It was lightly snowing outside. Mom was shocked to see me, and immediately let me in. I told her I was ready to come home. Who knows? She may have been enjoying her break from all of us, but she welcomed me back that day. We ate Japanese food and talked until bedtime. Mom asked me if I was prepared to take public transportation to school every day until I transferred schools. I said yes.

Mom and I settled into a routine, and I selfishly loved it with just the two of us. She was more relaxed than I'd ever experienced her, and we enjoyed one another's company. The time the two of us spent together during this period would be one of my most memorable with Mom. She became my closest friend. Mom taught me how to cook. We watched a lot of TV together.

It was then that I started assuming adult responsibilities to help her, and when I began to realize Mom didn't know everything. She was still a superwoman, but she was also human. It would be during this time with her that I would discover how much she didn't know, through no fault of her own. I developed a deep appreciation for how far Mom had come, from a naive young woman who had to teach herself to understand, speak, read and write the English language. I also gained a profound respect for the things we, as Americans often take for granted, both within our own country and in places where English is routinely taught as a second language.

Mom had always checked my homework. I had taken that for granted, but once I moved away from her, there was no one to do that for me. Returning home, I was glad I had Mom to review my work. It was during this time that I made a major discovery. One evening, after she'd reviewed my math and I double-checked something, I was surprised she didn't catch a glaring mistake I made.

In seventh grade, I was introduced to a new approach to math. I believe it was called "Infinite Math." I had just learned it, so it was highly unlikely she was aware of it, much less understood it. I thought about the many times when Mom would look at my homework, hand it back to me and ask, "Are you sure this is all correct?" I'd go back and double-check my work.

It was not until this day that I realized that there were likely times when she may not have had a clue what she was reviewing. As I thought more about it, I asked myself, "how would she know?" She'd only had an elementary school education.

Mom didn't know everything, and this realization somehow made me feel good to know she was human. I'm sure it had something to do with the way she expected perfection from me. It's difficult to explain my reaction, but when it dawned on me that she didn't know everything, I felt a sense of relief for myself and for her. But after that, I started looking more closely at my work instead of relying on her to check it.

In so many ways, Mom was superhuman. She possessed an incredible resourcefulness and could figure out how to fix almost anything. She could sew nearly anything with her bare hands and a needle and thread. I distinctly recall an occasion when Daddy made an impulsive purchase of an expensive daishiki (bright-colored tunic from West Africa) that he'd only worn once. Mom took that shirt, cut it up, and skillfully designed two of the most adorable matching halter tops for my sister and me. We loved them and proudly wore them out together. Mom was also conscious about recycling, but more out of necessity than concern for the environment or sustainability. I am still in awe of her.

Mom would never get any formal schooling in the US. There were many things she didn't understand, so even though I spoke very little Japanese, I sometimes assumed the role of translator for Mom. I went to doctors' appointments with her, listened to what they said, and explained what they said in ways she could understand. I taught myself how to file her tax returns. Fortunately, they were very uncomplicated. I tracked and renewed Mom's Alien or A-Number. The Alien Registration Number was used by the US Citizenship and Immigration Services to track immigrants in the US.

For some reason, Mom hated completing that Alien Form. Maybe it was that dreadful name, "alien." It would be many years later, but I believe Mom was in her sixties or possibly seventies when she took the test to become a US citizen and passed. She was elated, and I was so proud of her!

There were times when Mom received business paperwork that she didn't understand. I would review and research to provide her with options on what she needed to do. That timeframe was pre-Google, so I would sometimes have to go to the library to do research. This assisting Mom with adult stuff would become a recurring pattern throughout my teen years, and into my own adult life.

Mom and I lived in that apartment together for a while. Just the two of us. It was perfect. I never transferred schools, so I took the two buses from home to my junior high school every day until I graduated at the end of ninth grade. There seemed to be nothing unusual for this young teenager to travel across town to go to school. Overall, my home life was cool and stable.

During my junior high school years, making friends came more easily to me. I had developed a tendency to befriend those who, like me, didn't readily conform to societal molds. Perhaps it was because I empathized with their struggles. I knew all too well the process of starting anew and having to find my place in different environments.

I befriended two young classmates, Bonnie Villa and Mindy Jones. Bonnie was a smart, pretty Indian girl with a slight accent. Mindy was a shy, beautiful Black girl who transferred to our school midway through the year. Both seemed to have dispositions like mine. I don't recall my two friends being friends with one another, so this may have been over two separate periods of my junior high school experience. What I do know is that they both lived with their very strict fathers. I don't recall a mother's presence in either of their households.

I think Bonnie must have transferred out because I don't have any recollection of her presence in my last year or two of junior high school. Mindy and I became good friends. Mindy was shy, beautiful, goofy, and funny. Her older sister Cheryl embraced me like I was her little sister.

And just like I had done in elementary school, I would get up extra early and take the buses from South Philly to West Philly and go to Mindy's house in the morning so we could walk to school together. Until I wrote this, I had no idea that I had a pattern of doing this. I'm not even sure why I was doing it. After elementary school, I never attended a school in the neighborhood in which I lived. Maybe this pattern was my semblance of normalcy to just walk to school with my friends like most kids did. Who knows?

Mindy and I became good friends. Many students had grown up in that neighborhood and had been friends since elementary school. To them, we were outsiders. As a result, we were sometimes bullied. I remember a teacher, Miss G, whom I later learned was a member of the sorority of which I would eventually become a member (Alpha Kappa Alpha), though I did not have any clue what that was back then.

There was always some drama in junior high school, as was expected at that age. At one point, a group of girls wanted to fight Mindy and me. Surprisingly, Miss G. suggested that if we truly wanted to fight, we should bring our gym suits and settle it in the gym. Although I was sort of scared, I refused to back down. Mindy and I, as well as the other girls, engaged in a lot of posturing, but when given permission to fight, I don't think any of us really wanted to. We all eventually became friends.

During our final year of junior high, Mindy and I also befriended another girl named Belinda. Interestingly, the three of us became quite popular, which was a unique experience for me. It was a cool feeling to be hanging out with the "cool kids," and popularity offered some insulation from judgment and bullying. This time, instead of trying to fit in, we created our own crew—a group of friends who shared a bond and supported one another. We were all cute, dressed nicely, and were all friendly and interesting. I was happy with my social life.

After graduating from junior high school, my crew was

forced to split up. Both Mindy and Belinda ended up going to West Philly High. I was accepted into Overbrook High School's Scholars Magnet Program, so I was separated from my two best school friends from that point on. I was happy that they still had one another. The magnet program accepted students from across the city. I was once again faced with the dance of starting all over again. Fortunately, some of my junior high school classmates went to Overbrook as well. It was also around this time that Dad and Mom once again reconciled, and found a two-story, two-bedroom house within walking distance of our apartment. My Dad, brothers, and I all moved back together. It was my seventh move in my life, and I was only fifteen years old.

My parents never ended up transferring my baby brother Steven from his elementary school in West Philly to a school in our South Philly neighborhood. Consequently, Steven also took two buses from South Philly to his elementary school in West Philly each day. Steven did this commute alone from the age of seven. What prompted the change for him was that SEPTA, our local public transportation company, went on strike and Steven missed about a month's worth of school. He still passed his grade, but once his elementary school realized he didn't live in the neighborhood, he was transferred to a school in South Philly.

It wasn't long after our family moved into this house that Mom and Dad split up for good. I can't recall what signaled the final separation, but I know Dad was gone for good when I started high school. Mom's factory job gave her the ability to pay the bills all by herself, and to somehow stretch the money to do a little extra. The rest of our family lived in that little house in South Philly for longer than we lived anyplace else up to that point in my life. We lived there long enough to have developed friendships for life. Dad

45

contributed financial support, but Mom now knew she could handle it all if she had to, and she did.

My older brother Johnny joined the Army, so it was Mom, my baby brother Steven and me at home. Since Mom worked a full-time job and would come home tired, I managed the household, cooked, cleaned, ironed, did laundry, and did the grocery shopping. Having the oldest daughter assume the responsibility of managing the household chores was not uncommon in the Asian culture. Because my older sister had left for college at seventeen-years-old, those responsibilities fell to me.

Mom was the one bringing home the money, I was responsible for the upkeep of the home. Just like within many families I've observed within the African American culture, Japanese Moms treat their boys differently than they do their girls. My brothers' chores were only to dry and put away the dishes and take out the trash.

In high school, I commuted on public transportation for an hour and a half each way daily. I then came straight home and had dinner started before Mom came in from work at 3:45 pm. Her job was a twenty-minute bus ride away. After dinner and clean-up, I still had to do homework, study, and prepare for school the next day. Though it didn't dawn on me at the time, my mom was like a traditional Dad, and I was like a traditional Mom, while also being a full-time student. I never thought much about all the responsibility I had. I just know I didn't have the time or ability to do a lot of the things my friends and classmates who had more free time did. As a result, I had very little involvement in after-school activities.

Mom was very strict with all of her children. I can only speak about my experience, but I perceived Mom as most demanding of me. She had a very sharp tongue, and never felt she needed to hold back. There were times when I was just plain embarrassed at how she didn't mince her words. She was not always polite to friends I brought home. Consequently, I stopped inviting friends over. After they stopped coming, Mom accused me of being ashamed of her. Nothing could have been further from the truth. I was uncomfortable with my friends seeing how tough she was on me. It was somewhere around this time that I believe certain members of my family began to refer to me as a snob. How could I be a snob? I had nothing. I didn't give this issue too much thought. After all, I was a high school student now. I was excited and welcomed the challenge. I made friends with a lot of the other magnet students right away, beginning with the students who rode public transportation with me.

In my first semester, I also befriended someone who lived in my neighborhood. She was not a magnet student but was commuting to the school from South Philly like me.

She was older than me, pretty, hip, popular, and into things to which I had not yet been exposed. She introduced me to a whole crew of her older friends at the school. They were cool kids, and I liked being around them. I liked her and wanted her and her friends to like me too. I started hanging around her and her friends and doing the things they did. One activity was smoking pot in the mornings before school.

For that first semester, my routine was to meet them before 8 am, smoke with them, attend my first couple of classes (high), and then take a nap in my third-period class. This routine only lasted one semester. When I got my grades for that first quarter, everything changed. I saw letters on my report card I had never seen. I failed every subject except two, where I earned the lowest passing grade.

Other than my poor achievement test score fiasco from elementary school, I hadn't done anything this irresponsible in my entire life. I'm not sure why, but I was completely shocked at my grades. That day, that one-and-a-half-hour commute home was the longest trip ever, and I was filled with dread.

I recall feeling temporarily relieved that Daddy was no longer in the house, though I was much more afraid of Mom's reaction. I knew she would flip out, so I was wracking my brain trying to come up with good reasons to justify those grades.

As expected, after Mom saw the report card, she had a fit. She went off and told me how "disappointed" she was in me.

"No, please not that word." She'd used the "D" word.

Disappointed.

That word cut me like a knife. Didn't she know how disappointed I was in myself?

As it turned out, I didn't have to worry about giving Mom any excuses because she never asked. Just like the out-of-pattern behavior of my achievement test results, she never asked why. The thought never occurred to her that something could be off.

Mom saw those bad grades as a reflection on her as my mom, so they had to be fixed. Mom's punitive response when I was already disappointed in myself stayed with me. It wasn't rebellion, but a series of bad decisions, made day by day.

A few weeks earlier, Mom had given me a private phone line in my room. Cell phones were still decades away from being invented. It was a way for teenagers to enjoy some privacy. As punishment, Mom took away the phone. I was also grounded, although being grounded didn't affect me much since I didn't have much free time anyway.

My younger brother, Steven, had a joke ready for me. He said, "Hah! Your grades spell a palindrome." I'm not sure if I knew what a palindrome was before then. It was on that day that I learned a palindrome is a word, phrase, or sequence that reads the same backward as forward. Like the word "radar." I'll leave the grades that made up the palindrome to your imagination.

After receiving that report card, I promptly quit smoking pot and began to take my studies more seriously. However, it was difficult to dig myself out of that hole, and the grades would later come back to haunt me.

My grades for that first semester were so low and I had fallen so far behind that by the end of the school year, I was not able to raise my grades back to the average needed to remain in the Scholars program. I got kicked out of the magnet program and sent back to my neighborhood school in South Philly.

That following fall of my junior year, I went to my neighborhood school on the first day of school. I stood in front of the building but couldn't bring myself to walk into the school. After standing there for a while, I turned around and left. I just couldn't consider the prospect of starting over at another high school. I loved Overbrook.

I decided to go back to Overbrook, praying with a sense of desperation during the entire trip. Once I got there, I used my best persuasion skills. I'm sure there was some begging and pleading and somehow, I was able to remain at Overbrook, though I could not remain in the Scholars Magnet program. I was so grateful and promised myself that I would never again allow my strong need to belong to put my future in jeopardy.

The balance of my experience at Overbrook High School was truly wonderful, and it represented yet another major transformational period. Throughout my life, I have had more than my fair share of insecurities. If I'm honest, I still do. Physically, I was considered funny-looking, and so skinny that my siblings nicknamed me "Bones." I had a knack for finding poison ivy wherever I went, even tiny patches in wide-open fields, earning me the nickname "Bumps." My wild, curly hair was a constant mess since my Japanese mother, with her bone-straight hair didn't know how to manage mine. I was always extremely nearsighted, needing glasses for as long as I can remember.

In middle school, I was flat-chested compared to my peers. I also went through junior high, high school, and my freshman year of college with a chipped tooth after that fight with my older brother. And the list goes on. It's surprising I had any confidence at all, right? Once I was no longer in the Magnet program, Overbrook assigned me to classes that were not as challenging for me. But considering all the responsibilities I had at home, I admit I was okay with coasting.

Feel free to judge me.

And yes, my poor high school freshman choices would come back to haunt me sooner than I thought. I think it was in my senior year of high school that I tried to run for a school office. I didn't know that the student cabinet looked at your grades as part of the criteria. I was disqualified because of my grades in the first semester of my freshman year. More hurtful was the chatter among some of my peers that I was dumb. I knew I was smart but had just made bad decisions. I accepted my fate. I was grateful to still be on the senior cabinet, on which I served proudly.

One of the best things about attending Overbrook was that it was up the street from my paternal Grandmother's house, whom I also called "Mom." My relationship with my grandmother was truly special. Probably because my parents called her Mom, I grew up calling her Mom. I adored her. She was beautiful, stylish, classy, very feisty, and yes - had a mean streak to her. But she was a loving and doting grandmother in every sense of the word to me.

Because she lived so close to my high school, Mom would pick me up from school when I would experience cramps too painful to stay in school. She would bring me to her house, let me take a nap, give me aspirin, feed me, and put me on the bus to go home. I valued those afternoons for several reasons. One, my grandmother babied me during those times, and two: they were the few days I was excused from having to be home and having dinner ready by the time my mom came home. Mom took me on vacations and did things with me that she didn't do with my siblings. I was well-behaved, cute, got good grades, and didn't say much. In the era of "children should be seen and not heard," I was winning! As I looked back on it as an adult, Mom's favoring me was probably unfair, and led to resentment I would later experience from some family members.

Yet another (oftentimes conflicting) duality existed within me as I also filled two very distinct roles in my relationship with my mom during my teen years. On the one hand, I struggled with meeting extremely high expectations she seemed to have, of only me. She was a very strict mother whom I felt expected perfection from me. She expected perfect grades, discouraged me from dating and imposed curfews more rigid than those of any of my friends.

But on the other hand, Mom oftentimes treated me like I was the adult, relied on me, and placed a lot of responsibility on me. At a young age I assumed a more adult role in caring for Mom which would continue throughout my adult life. I embraced this responsibility and even prided myself on my ability to solve

51

problems and get stuff done!

Later in life, I would learn about a term that described my situation: "parentification." This term was first coined by Hungarian American psychiatrist Ivan Boszormenyi-Nagy, one of the founders of the field of family therapy. "Parentification occurs when the roles of parent and child are reversed."

Understandably, I had a better command of the English language, so I assisted with business-related matters. Mom also used me as a sounding board and sometimes gave me more information than a teenager needed to have or know about what she was going through. The combination of all the physical and emotional support I provided oftentimes put me more in the role of a caregiver. This was a role for which I was not always mature enough, nor prepared, but I did what Mom needed, without argument.

For the most part, I'd taken this balancing act in stride. Looking back on it, I can only say it was a lot. It also created expectations that would challenge me long after I left home, got married and had my own children.

I was not the only one in my family who'd assumed this role. When I was younger, my older sister cared for and cooked for us. It was when she left for college at the age of seventeen, and my parents split up for good that my "parentification" really began. In addition to the housekeeping duties, I accompanied Mom to doctors' appointments, handled a lot of Mom's business, wrote letters for her, and made phone calls on her behalf.

The two distinct roles undoubtedly created confusion and challenges for me as I navigated between them. Layer onto that the mood swings teenage girls go through. You get the drift. For my part, I also know I wasn't always the easiest daughter to raise.

This heavy reliance on me also influenced how much responsibility I would later assume for others, resulting in what appeared to be a natural need to take care of others. It probably wasn't.

I grew up feeling that my needs were not as important as others.' When I was older and learned more about the concept of parentification, I began to understand myself and my mother so much better.

I think the most significant result early in my life was the further confirmation that I had only myself on whom to depend. I sincerely believe my parents did the very best they could. But I never felt confident enough to trust them, or anyone else to take care of me. I developed this self-reliance that often served me well, but also hurt me at times.

While I provided emotional support for Mom, she was not always able to do so for me. I didn't feel it was emotionally safe to share mistakes, risks, failures, or even fears with her, so I seldom did. Honestly, I rarely shared any of my challenges, mistakes or failures with any of my family members.

Despite our challenges, I hold such great memories of Mom and me during those teen years. On Thursdays after work for her, and school for me, Mom and I would meet at the Gallery, the downtown mall. We would have dinner, and then she would buy me a new outfit. This was during that stage where, the funny-looking duckling began to transform physically. I went from funny-looking, to cute. Because I had a unique look, it garnered curious stares from others. I was like a chameleon, so whatever environment in which I found myself, I blended in. When Asians looked at me, they saw Asian. Black people saw Black-something. Latino people saw Spanish.

We are a bit more politically correct now, but back then, I was constantly asked the question: "What are you?" Mom loved the attention my "unfigureoutableness" generated, and by today's standards, I was often overdressed for a teenager. However, that's how we "Brook" women rolled. My high school had a reputation for being best-dressed, and it was during this time that I began noticing how my uniqueness became an asset. I mentioned earlier how my combination of achievement, intelligence, physical beauty, and kindness made me stand out. I was realizing the impact on others, but from a young age, maintained a strong need for people to see me as smart, first and foremost. Mom made sure I knew proper meal etiquette, and we spent considerable time talking about current events. Mom took pride in "schooling me" on the dos and don'ts for proper young ladies. She'd also assess men and boys who would be checking me out, creating scenarios that were entertaining and oftentimes probably far-fetched, telling me what to look for, and what to avoid. Those dinner dates with Mom were special times for both of us, and I'm grateful for the memories.

Next Up:
College

It was during this time that I began setting my sights on college, so I was focused on getting my grades and GPA as high as possible. I loved attending Overbrook High School. By now, I had a great set of friends, and I was growing more popular.

So many things changed during my senior year, and all I could think about was going away to college. When I told Mom I needed to get involved in extracurricular activities to improve my chances of getting into the colleges I wanted, she agreed. That took some pressure off me to have to rush home every day to prepare dinner, as I stayed after school more often.

I didn't know anything about parentification and its impact on me back then. I just knew that as I got closer to my senior year of high school graduation, there was one thing I was most certainly going to do. I was going to attend college, far away from home. I would love to say I aspired to attend college to advance myself, receive further training, or pursue my professional dreams. The truth was, by this time, I just wanted to go to college to get a break from all the responsibility I had at home.

Howard University and Penn State were the only two schools in which I was interested. Because my dad came of age in an era where many believed that "white was better," he told me he would not pay for me to go to a Historically Black College.

Consequently, my only option was Penn State. Because neither of my parents went to college, nor did their parents, my understanding of my options was limited. I didn't know much about other colleges, and I had no idea what an Ivy League school was.

I did all the work myself applying to schools, as well as applying for financial aid and scholarships. I got accepted into Penn State, main campus, and I did pretty well securing financial aid.

My senior year of high school was likely the best year of my life up to that point. I met my very first boyfriend. We were considered a popular couple.

I went on my senior trip, attended the senior prom, was an assistant editor of the yearbook, and I was on the senior cabinet. My boyfriend was selected Prom King from a drawing. It was the first year that the prom king's date was not automatically named the prom queen as in the previous year the prom king drawn had a date who didn't attend the school. We voted this year to use the lottery system to hold drawings for both prom king and queen. How about that for luck?

But the ultimate and ironic highlight that year was at my twelfth-grade graduation. I was presented with the District Four's "Two Hours of Excellence" award, along with a plaque and a huge trophy. Created by Reverend Jesse Jackson, this distinction was awarded to the student who'd made the most significant improvements in their grades over the course of their high school years.

So what I'd been able to make such a drastic improvement from my freshman year because my classes were not as challenging? Don't judge me for accepting it. I met the criteria.

Mom kept that big trophy for years, moving it around with

her for as long as she could. She still had the plaque among her things when she died several months ago. It now hangs in my office.

I had some concerns about how my mom would manage once I left home to go to college, but once I stepped foot on that campus, it became all about me. The great news? Mom would manage just fine without me.

For my first semester at Penn State, Daddy paid the remaining amount owed on my tuition after scholarships, grants, and any other financial aid I received. He paid two hundred and thirty-eight dollars. That would be the only payment he would ever have to make during my time at Penn State.

My goal in going away to college was to be free from all the responsibility I had at home. It mattered less where I went. What was important was that I would only be responsible for myself and completing the requirements for my degree.

I saw college as my emancipation. And no, I'm not ashamed to admit it. I had an amazing, life-changing freshman year at Penn State. The things other students took for granted were exciting novelties for me.

In college, there was unlimited cafeteria food that I didn't have to prepare or clean up after I was done. Because Mom didn't like salad, we never ate it at home. I discovered that I loved salad and was ecstatic that I could take as many trips as I wanted to the salad bar. Unlike most students, I loved dorm food! And it showed in that first year.

And who knew you could gain so much weight eating salad? My "Freshman Ten" (pound) weight gain was more like "Freshman Twenty." Because I was so thin, I welcomed the extra pounds. I resolved that I would do well in college, for many of the wrong reasons, but so what? In college, there was no curfew, and no one who cared what I did. By now, I made friends easily. Some of my Overbrook classmates attended Penn State, so there were people familiar to me. I was so happy! And it was the beginning of my truly coming into my own.

University Park, Penn State's main campus is in the middle of nowhere. For many of my Black friends and fellow students, it was a bit of a culture shock. Some of my close friends didn't like the isolation. The attrition rate was high among African American students. Some friends never returned after the first trimester. Others transferred to other schools, or never returned after our freshman year.

I found my crew, and I also met students who would become friends for life. I met my Cindy right away. Neither one of us recalls how we met, but it feels to me like Cindy and I have always known one another. She was such an instrumental part of my college experience that it just felt like she was always there. Cindy was smart as a whip. She was fun, had a great sense of humor, and was warm and kind.

Back then, she kicked everybody's butt in chess, always gracefully. There was an aura about Cindy that was so confident. I wanted to learn how to exude that same elegant, smart confidence she had. She was calm and cool. Cindy quickly became my best friend.

I wonder if she recalls that time shortly after we met when I called her room after midnight one night and asked her to go downtown with me for ice cream. She replied: "I'm in my pajamas, ready for bed." I was about to say: "Okay, bye." But she then said, "Give me five minutes to change, and I'll be ready." I knew right then and there that Cindy was my kind of people. And at that moment she became my soul sister. We became Sigma Sweethearts together, and where you saw one, you saw the other. We have a whole bunch of stories, but those go to the grave with us! Cindy is still in my life now, and I am so grateful for her friendship.

I also met my other college best friend, Marcine, in our building's cafeteria in the first few months. She and I are still a part of one another's lives.

Ironically, the girl who beat me up in sixth grade? Our paths would again cross. I'm sure she remembered the fight. We never talked about it. I was by then in a different place, killing it in college, enjoying every aspect of campus life, confident, popular, pretty, and I had a great group of what would become life-long friends.

During my freshman year, Cindy and Marcine, along with other friends, threw me my first birthday party ever. It was a total surprise. I still recall my shock, and how special I felt. Growing up, I had thrown parties for my family members. This was the first time someone had done this for me.

Freshman year flew by. I returned to Philly for the summer. I had secured a paid internship with a government agency, but it didn't start for another month. I took a job at McDoogal's in a rough neighborhood for a month. I must have looked like an easy target because I got robbed twice in the first two weeks. As a result, I requested to be taken off the cash register. Consequently, my job for the following and last two weeks was to cook breakfast and lunch food. I smelled like McDoogal's fries every day. I swear that was one of the hardest jobs I'd ever worked. I was exhausted when I got home each day. Can I tell you how happy I was when my internship with the Government started? At the same time, I developed a lifelong respect and appreciation for people who work in fast food establishments. It's hard work.

That summer, I earned rent money for the apartment Marcine and I planned to share in my sophomore year, as well as the money I needed to become a member of Alpha Kappa Alpha Sorority during my sophomore year.

With my very first paycheck from McDoogal's, I got my front chipped tooth fixed. Then Mom bought me contact lenses, so I no longer had to wear prescription glasses. With the weight I'd gained in my freshman year, my hips had rounded out, making my shape look less like a boy's.

That summer, I also committed to a lifetime of practicing Buddhism. From then on, no matter what was going on, I made sure I did my prayers twice a day, every day. I returned to Penn State that fall with a whole new look and an increased level of self-confidence. Back then, I don't recall us wearing make-up every day the way many college students do today, so what you saw was what you got.

For me, repairing the tooth and losing the glasses made the biggest difference. I noticed right away that guys started looking at me differently. I can't recall who, but someone said that beauty is indeed a curse when that is the only thing people remember or recall about you. Natural beauty is something over which we have little control. Although for the right price today, you can get nearly anything done to make you beautiful: hair, face, teeth, skin, body, etc.

But even if you have the means to do all that, the worst thing is when that's all they see when they look at you. No matter who you are, beauty fades over time. What did I want people to value about me? The way I made them feel. My impact on their lives. To me, the time and care I give others, as well as understanding, acceptance, empathy and authenticity are what truly matter.

Unfortunately, we don't look that deeply when we meet people. While I appreciated some of the advantages of my developing beauty, it was much more important to me that people knew that I was caring and smart.

So many things fell into place during my sophomore year. Cindy, Marcine and I would go through one of our most memorable collective experiences of our lives together. We were all initiated into our sorority, Alpha Kappa Alpha together, along with three other amazing women.

I can't explain the happiness and sense of belonging I felt when I was initiated into my beloved sorority. I knew then, and I know even more now, that becoming a member of Alpha Kappa Alpha was one of the best decisions I've made in my life.

My junior and senior years were equally as wonderful. College was one of the best periods of my life. I always say Penn State offers anything you want. It is a world in and of itself. I can only speak for my own undergraduate and graduate school experiences, but I think college offers young people the best opportunity to experiment and do whatever it is they want to do. At Penn State I found acceptance. Though my crew primarily consisted of Black people and Black organizations, I also met so many others along the way.

At the beginning of my last trimester, which I thought would be an opportunity for me to coast, I learned that I didn't have enough credits to graduate that spring. I had to get special department approval to take a class-load above the maximum credits allowed, as I could not afford to stay for another semester. I was successful in getting the approval and took a full load of classes.

To pay my rent, I had to maintain my waitressing job at a nightclub. That last semester was very stressful, and I couldn't even think about life post-graduation. My parents were making plans for their second and last trip to Penn State for graduation, and I couldn't disappoint them. Fortunately, I graduated on time that spring.

Then life took an unexpected turn. Around the time I graduated, I experienced a horrible series of events that changed my life. They happened at a time when I should have been looking forward to the next big step in my life as a college graduate. Back then, for many of us first-generation college graduates, the goal was to get that degree. Unlike many of today's college graduates who routinely secure multiple job offers before graduation, many of my friends and I used graduation as the jumping-off point to begin looking for employment.

I returned to Philadelphia and my mother's home, with neither a job nor any prospects. That in and of itself was not a great situation, but it was further compounded by the unexpected events that occurred. I was shaken and didn't feel comfortable sharing what happened with anyone. I didn't have the type of relationship with my mother where I could confide in her, so I suffered in silence.

I could easily write a book about that period of my life, and the downsides of suffering in silence. What happened is not germane to this story, except that it further eroded my confidence in placing trust in others.

Once back home, I barely made it through the days. I went back to my former routine of cooking, cleaning, and taking care of my family. That was probably the best thing for me to do as I struggled to process life through different lenses. It was actually a welcome distraction. I began to lean heavily on my Buddhist practice to get through this and create my path ahead. I determined to create my new kintsugi, taking the broken pieces of my life and putting them back together in a way that would be even better than that which I was leaving behind.

As I knew I needed to just take a deep breath and get back out there, I decided to start small. I soon found myself reconnecting with my Buddhist practice and family, reconnecting with my friends, and re-starting my adult life in Philly. I got a job in retail to get myself back into a routine. I liked the job, though I knew it was a temporary stop. I decided Law School might be a good next step, and in my spare time prepped for and took the Law School Admission Test.

In a remarkably short period of time, I found myself feeling happy again, and very optimistic. I attribute my healing to my Buddhist practice.

Shortly thereafter I learned of an opportunity to earn my Master of Public Administration degree at Penn State. It was a brand-new degree program, and if I were accepted, my full tuition would be paid.

I applied to the program and was accepted. Penn State also accepted my LSAT scores and awarded me a full scholarship as well as a stipend to cover my living expenses. I was ecstatic, though there was one obstacle in the way at that time.

I trust the universe to guide me more than I trust my own mind. Here's why. I believe we are constantly getting signs from the universe that drop "breadcrumbs" leading us to and away from certain directions. The challenge is in our ability and willingness to recognize the signs. When I am at a crossroads, I always think prayer first. Sometimes I get answers that I want to interpret to support the path I want to take.

You know those red flags you convince yourself you don't see? Or worse, ignore? Or the answers that are glaring down at you, but since they're not the answers you want, you disregard them? Yes, those.

Fortunately, I put my faith first and pray to know the best option when this happens. I'd never thought about pursuing a master's in public administration until it was casually mentioned to me that I apply for this new program. The offer of a full scholarship and monthly stipend to cover expenses sweetened the deal for sure.

At the same time, a friend in Philly was helping me to land a job. It was a newly created position that would have kept me in Philly. Thus, I would have had to choose between accepting a scholarship to earn my master's degree or taking a better-paying job in Philly. While I knew that I had to consider my long-term success and thus should pursue the advanced degree, I also wanted the job that was being created specifically for me. It was the result of my mother working (conspiring) with a dear friend, as neither one of them wanted me to leave Philly at that time. Each had their reasons.

Of course, I wanted the job and the instant gratification. Though I was praying for the right answer, deep down I wanted to take the job. Had the universe not slapped me hard on the head with obvious signs, I would have taken the job. As it turned out, news broke of a major investigation of the organization that was going to hire me. Even if I still wanted to take the job, hiring me was among the lowest priorities for this organization. It now found itself in a position where it had to focus on much bigger issues. I saw the job that I was hoping to get disintegrate before my eyes.

So I packed all my things and went back to Penn State to pursue my master's degree.

Though Mom didn't want me to go to graduate school, she helped me to get my stuff together and did her best to support me. My dad told me she'd cried the entire way home when they took me up to Penn State for my freshman year. She never returned until my undergraduate graduation. She didn't want me to go back. I'm sure she didn't want to go through that again. My dad and brother drove me back to Penn State. As I had to scramble at the last minute, I rented an efficiency, sight unseen. When we walked into my new place, I was first excited and then horrified.

As soon as we opened the door, we were overwhelmed by the strong odor of a recent visit from the exterminator, and there were bugs, literally hundreds of them all over the apartment. Most of them were already dead or near death. Daddy and Johnny helped me clean them all out and we then went to grab dinner before the two of them got on the road to go home. When we got back from dinner, I said goodbye to them at the door, and then went into my apartment. To my horror, there were hundreds of new bugs there that had seemingly come in from the walls in that short time we were at dinner. Anyone who knows me well knows that I am deathly afraid of bugs, and will call anyone, at any time and ask them to drop what they are doing to remove a bug.

Cell phones hadn't yet been invented. Only landlines were available then, and I didn't yet have my phone connected in my apartment. I ran to the pay phone outside and called my mom, nearly in tears. Mom told me to just try to get through the night and get on the bus the next morning and come back home. She would arrange to get my stuff home later. I recall asking her, incredulously, "You mean like get my stuff and leave school?"

"Yes," she replied. "Your dad and brother can go back up and get your stuff later." Mom was dead serious.

All you need to do is give this determined woman the easy way out to get her to stiffen her upper lip and figure out a way to fight through. That's exactly what I did. I went to the store and got a can of bug spray and sprayed it all around the perimeter of a chair. I sat in that chair all night, keeping my feet off the floor.

I swept the bugs and scooped them into the toilet, flushing the toilet easily five times afterward. I repeated that several times during that night. Where were they continuing to come from?

The next morning, I called the rental office, made a huge fuss, and threatened them. They came out and exterminated the place again the next day. I also demanded they exterminate the apartments on either side of me, as well as the one above me.

In the week that followed, I'd inhaled so many fumes that I lost my appetite, which would not return for weeks. This resulted in a significant amount of weight loss that first semester. But I got through it, and never saw another bug in my apartment.

Bug problem aside, I smile now as I relive that excitement I felt back then. I had my own apartment and was living alone for the first time in my life, at the age of twenty-five. For a graduate student with very little money, I decorated my place beautifully with furniture mostly from the local "Five and Dime" stores. This apartment was all mine. Having my own place gave me lots of alone time. I discovered that I absolutely loved my solitude. When I felt overwhelmed, I would shut myself in to decompress. I had the best balance of study, prayer time, reading, sleeping and socializing. It was the beginning of one of the happiest and most peaceful phases of my life. In the true spirit of Kintsugi, I'd managed to rebuild my shattered life into a more beautiful, inspiring, and hopeful one.

Graduate school would provide yet another incredibly transformational experience for me. Being back up at Penn State as a graduate student made me feel very much like a real grown-up. It also allowed me to redefine my experience at the place where I'd found myself. That horrible experience just one year ago had negatively colored the end of my undergrad experience. This was my opportunity to create a new and positive experience at my alma mater.

My confidence was at an all-time high. I felt smart, determined, industrious, and unstoppable! In addition to having my own place, I had money to handle my monthly expenses, plus a little extra spending money. A couple of my sorority sisters and friends from my undergrad days were still at Penn State so I had folks with whom I could hang.

I quickly met and befriended fellow graduate students, and I loved this amazing, brand-new master's program. Once there, I knew I was guided to the right path for my life. Now having the benefit of reflection, I also realize just how naive and downright clueless I was as well. Don't get me wrong. Cluelessness is not always necessarily a bad thing. But when I look back on some situations in my life where a little more self-awareness and awareness of others would've worked to my benefit, graduate school was one.

One such time was in dealing with an overly friendly professor. Looking back now, I acknowledge that he'd shown signs of having an interest in me, and at times, his actions were a little odd, like complimenting me in front of the class. Back then this was nothing that I considered to be out of order. By today's standards, it would likely be perceived as inappropriate.

This wasn't the first time I'd encountered a situation like

this, so I was in a slightly better position to recognize it for what it was. I recalled an experience from a different point in my undergraduate college career where a professor recruited a handful of us students to work on a special project outside of the class for extra credit and money. He'd secured a research grant to conduct a study and we students would help to collect the necessary data. I jumped at the chance. We all traveled together to another city, and all stayed in a local hotel. As soon as we arrived, we attended orientation and training. We then went back to our hotel rooms and settled in, agreeing to meet later for dinner at a certain time. I came out of my room for dinner at the same time he came out of his room, which was coincidentally right next to mine. I didn't think anything of it. Why would I? This was my professor.

Our group went to dinner, and afterward, we went back to the hotel and he and I struck up a conversation in the hall. We chatted for a minute or two and then I said, good night and went to my room. As I look back on it now, there is a chance he may have had other motives, but my cluelessness probably prevented him from making an advance. I wouldn't be surprised if he had made an advance, but I didn't recognize it. He was probably not that much older than I was. But back then, I'd viewed professors in a different light, and the thought of dating a professor, especially one who had control over my grades, never once entered my mind. So, I never even connected any dots. I'm truly not sure there were even dots to connect.

It wasn't until the end of the semester that I was forced to question his motives. One of my classmates was complaining to me and other students about how much she disliked him. I simply said, "I thought he was pretty cool." She mentioned that she didn't believe he graded her fairly and directly asked me what grade he gave me. I replied: "I earned an A in the class."

"Of course you did," she replied. "We all noticed how he hit on you all semester." I was completely floored. This was said, not only around me but in the company of some of our other classmates as well. I brushed it off at that moment, but it irritated the hell out of me. The insinuation that I didn't deserve the grade was what I focused on. But as I looked back on it, there were certain things that I realized that may have been perceived differently. I prided myself on being approachable and friendly, and I would (and still will) talk to almost anyone. Should I have presented myself in a less friendly manner?

The possibility that someone like a professor might be interested in me was so far-fetched that it just would not have registered as a possibility. At that time, even though I thought I was grown, I was still only twenty-something years old compared to a professor. And I never fully grasped the attention my different look garnered. Though I knew I was considered attractive, I never used my looks to curry additional favor.

And I hated when folks automatically dismissed my intelligence. That was what made me the most upset about my interaction with my classmate. I also hated the reference to the "we," in "we noticed," which we sometimes use to lend credibility to what we are saying. It implies "It's not just me who noticed it." And it can bring on a paranoia that makes us question: "Am I the only one who didn't see it?"

Life went on, but the life lesson stuck.

"Shiranu ga hotoke" - The English translation is "Ignorance is bliss."

What I never picked up from my professor likely helped us both to avert an awkward situation. That's a situation where I am okay with ignorance being bliss. In addition to what I learned from the curriculum, I learned some valuable life lessons as well. I also realized I had to be more diligent in reading signs and situations.

As a graduate student with more awareness facing this situation again, I handled it differently. This now confident and less naïve graduate student adopted and communicated my self-imposed policy that I would not sleep where I studied, nor where I ate.

The reality was that I had very little control over my looks, but always wondered why there was so much focus placed on them. How about we talk about my brain? How about the fact that I am empathetic, smart, funny, sensitive, unselfish and many other characteristics at which I work hard? And I challenge you to find anyone who knows me who would deny that I am a very hard worker.

Don't get me wrong. There were plenty of benefits and dare I say, privileges afforded me because of my different look and multiracial ethnicity. A highlight was having my photo featured in a university-wide marketing campaign designed to showcase the university's commitment to recruiting diverse students. Penn State launched a targeted recruitment campaign aiming to attract students from diverse racial backgrounds. My picture was chosen, along with three others. The campaign's promotional material was widely distributed across our many campuses. Had my dear friend, former college classmate, and Penn State recruiter Mike Phillips not mentioned it to me at one of our Black Alumni reunions many years later, I would have never known that my photo was used in this initiative. To prove it to me, he took a picture of my picture, as well as the three others hanging on the wall in the office building where he worked. I only learned about this campaign decades later.

A framed copy of this picture proudly sits in my office today. I am especially proud of this campaign and my involvement as it was used to inspire others.

It was also during this time that I met and fell in love with a fellow graduate student. He was tall, dark, handsome, funny and smart. He was so confident it blew me away. Some called him arrogant. I loved every bit of it. I hadn't ever dated anyone so self-assured. He'd gotten his undergrad degree from a Historically Black College/University (HBCU), and up to that point, I'd only heard about that "unique confidence" instilled in graduates of HBCUs. As I got to know him, I began to understand exactly what they were talking about.

Dating him was in a word, intoxicating. I probably shouldn't share that I only started dating him to get back at someone he was dating, who was a side chick of an old flame of mine. But I fell madly in love with him. I learned so much from him, and we had so much fun together. I was due to finish my graduate work a year before him. He warned me not to get too serious as he'd confessed that he had some baggage from earlier long-distance relationships and that once I left Penn State, our relationship would have to end. "I take no prisoners…" he said. Of course, I didn't believe him. We had such a great relationship that I thought we would last forever. I would soon find out that he meant what he said.

We dated until I completed my coursework and had only my thesis to complete. I could do that from anywhere, so I returned to Philly to work part-time and complete this final requirement. I was sad to leave Penn State, but excited to begin this new phase of my life. My time in graduate school was short but amazing, and now it was time to get a job and go out in the real world. This time I was so ready, except I didn't want to leave this man who'd introduced me to a love I'd never before experienced.

Within weeks after moving back to Philly, I'd gotten a job recruiting students for an Art and Fashion school while I completed my master's thesis. I liked the job and was happy that it paid enough to allow me to move out of Mom's house. Within weeks of moving back to Philly, I found a place to stay.

I didn't expect the reaction from Mom, who didn't speak to me for several months after I moved out. She'd thought I would live at home for a while and things would go back to the way they'd been before I left for grad school. Sadly, she felt abandoned.

I moved into a house owned by my sorority sister and former college roommate, Marcine and her cousin Robbin. The rent was doable, and the arrangement was perfect. Marcine was already like family, and I immediately grew to love Robbin. It was a great arrangement.

I resolved to fix things with Mom once I was settled with my new job, new home and my roommates. It was a great move that worked well for us all. I quickly settled into a routine that consisted of schoolwork, hanging out with roommates and friends on the weekends. Their grandmother and Marcine's father accepted me as part of the family.

I once again immersed myself into my Buddhist practice. My roommates worried that I was a part of a cult, but the more I leaned into my practice, the better life got for me. I was happy with nearly every aspect of my life. Mom eventually started talking to me again, and the roomies' fears of my being part of a cult were allayed as they learned more about my religion, and they saw my life blossom.

However, the man with whom I was madly in love started ghosting me before "ghosting" was a thing. I kept pursuing him because I simply did not believe he was breaking up with me. During the first few months I spent considerable time vacillating between trying to change his mind and nursing my broken heart. Over time, I began accepting that we were done, stopped reaching out to him, and eventually moved on.

Interestingly, after receiving his MBA he accepted a job, moved to Philly, and reached out to me. At first, I was excited as I'd hoped he and I could pick up where we left off.

We went out a few times, but so many things were different this time. When we're in love, we often wear these convenient blinders, but as the infatuation fades, our vision becomes clearer. And eventually, I saw things I hadn't didn't seen before. I realized that he was the same smart, funny handsome man, but I was now different.

During the infatuation stage, I filled in gaps with what I wanted to see. It wasn't his fault I did that. I was the one projecting my desires onto him. He was still an awesome man, but I realized that we were just too fundamentally different from one another.

It also became crystal clear that he never felt the same way about me as I did about him. I was surprised by my comfort with letting the relationship go. My roommates were shocked when I shared this realization with them. They knew how much I had cared for him and expected me to be ecstatic when he moved to my city.

I'd also experienced some guilt because he shared that I was one of the reasons he'd accepted the job in Philly. I didn't immediately end whatever it was we were doing. I've always struggled with letting people down or letting people go.

I just started taking longer to return his calls, stopped making plans, and eventually stopped making myself available. I knew he'd eventually get the message.

As I've grown older and hopefully a bit wiser, I've learned that it is far more compassionate to be direct and honest. Letting things linger, or worse, ghosting, only makes it harder on not one, but both parties.

The final sign came when he kept pressing me to come over one Saturday night, saying he really needed to talk. He promised that afterward, I would understand everything. I was at home, ready to unwind and spend a quiet evening alone. But I said: "Okay." As I was getting dressed, he called back.

"Wear a trench coat with nothing on underneath," he said. "Sorry, what did you just say?"

Did I hear him correctly? I was at a loss for words.

He repeated, "Wear a trench coat with nothing on underneath."

I, at a loss for words, murmured, "Uh, okay…" and hung up. Seriously, did I hear that right? I replayed the conversation in my mind several times. I had to laugh. Here I was, done with the relationship and comfortable with my decision. Yet, I felt bad about letting him go. I actually felt sorry for him. Mind you — this is the same person who ghosted me for months. I'm not sure why, but the last thing I expected was that he only wanted a booty call.

And just like that, closing that chapter became a much easier decision. I called him back, and on the phone, we parted ways gracefully and amicably. I like to think I have done this with almost every ending of a relationship. We remained friends until his untimely death about a decade ago.

Adulting:
Navigating Corporate America and Dating

After that experience, I took a break from dating. I was focused on my new life as a grown woman, finishing my thesis and building my career.

I'd done the pivot and "fitting in" dance so many times by this point in my life that I felt comfortable with it. I always saw my natural ability to code-switch as a major strength. I could speak well enough, present myself sufficiently, and read people and situations well. What I wasn't prepared for at that point was my need to fit in "psycho-professionally." I'm not sure if I made up that term, but it was learning to adapt my mindset around certain values I held close from my cultural conditioning.

After about a year at the Art and Fashion College, I had my sights set on Bell of Pennsylvania (now Verizon), but in an informal interview, I was told I would greatly enhance my employment chances if I first got some industry sales and telecommunications experience.

My next move was to join a small telecommunications company, MCI to jumpstart my career. It didn't take long for me to realize how much I enjoyed the corporate environment and that I had a knack for sales. After nine months at MCI, I formally applied to Bell of Pennsylvania, which marked the beginning of what would become one of the most rewarding professional experiences of my life.

The people with whom I worked at Bell were undeniably some of the brightest individuals I had encountered up to that point in my life. As a manager in my first job, they referred to me as an "off-the-streeter" because I had not grown up within the Bell system. Soon after I was hired, they hired an amazing young Black woman who would become one of my dearest friends, Patsy. This woman possessed intelligence, education, charm, and a great sense of humor. Most importantly, she exuded confidence and authenticity. Her ability to effortlessly navigate various professional and social situations and communicate with virtually anyone inspired me. I made it my goal to emulate her style.

I closely watched Patsy, particularly as she seamlessly transitioned between formal and informal styles as the situation warranted. It wasn't easy for me to switch between different styles at that point. What I discovered was that Patsy possessed an innate ability to read people and respond accordingly. Despite being only a few years older than me, her level of maturity was far superior to mine. Patsy's emotional intelligence complemented her intellectual capabilities. She became a trusted friend whom I knew really cared about me and my success, and never appeared to have any ulterior motives. When she coached me, I listened. We became such good friends that years later she would be a bridesmaid at my wedding. I hate that we lost contact over the years, as Patsy was most definitely a keeper.

I participated in professional development programs whenever I had the opportunity. When I tell people that I was painfully shy as a youngster, they don't believe me. I would not have believed I'd eventually be comfortable communicating with anyone about nearly anything. Preparation and practice were my primary keys to success. More importantly, I learned that I had a voice, and that people were genuinely interested in hearing what I had to say.

One program that significantly enhanced my communication skills was Toastmasters. I cannot overstate how much I loved Toastmasters. I eagerly awaited our weekly sessions and actively participated whenever possible. Not only did I enjoy it, but I also consistently excelled in the competitions.

I recall one Toastmasters session when I won a competition against someone who invoked the "emotion" speech. This type of speech is nearly always a good idea because you often get extra sympathy points when you tell a sad story. My opponent told a story about someone dealing with cancer. It was good, as was mine, but my prepared speech was about parking tickets! Yet, I still won the competition. After the session, I went to the restroom and overheard two co-workers in the private stalls talking back and forth to one another. They didn't know I was in one of the stalls. One commented, "Boy, that Barbara Lee sure is a great speaker, isn't she?"

"Yes, she is" replied the other. "I understand she is Japanese." Well, ain't that a blip? I resisted the urge to disguise my voice and say: "she's also African American." Instead, I chuckled to myself, washed my hands, and slipped out of the restroom before they knew I was there. That speech and a few subsequent ones caught the attention of someone who would later become extremely instrumental in my professional growth. She will never know how much.

A little over a year into my tenure at Bell, I was approached about a seemingly fantastic promotion opportunity. I vividly recall the interview with the individual who would later become the head of our new venture. Linda Waddell was a lovely, petite, brilliant, powerful, and charming white woman. The head of the department I currently worked in, Linda was promoted and charged with developing a new game-changing concept for the company. She was in the process of assembling her team from scratch. I couldn't believe she was considering me for a role in her group!

Walking into her office, my attention was immediately drawn to her Mensa sign, which didn't surprise me. Mensa is an international organization comprised of members with very high IQ scores. And then I saw another sign that read: "I know I'm brilliant, tell me I'm beautiful."

Filled with excitement and nervousness, I couldn't believe this larger-than-life woman wanted to talk to me! During our conversation, she explained the responsibilities of the job. I would be providing technical training and developing a sales strategy for a new concept called electronic mail, which involved computer-based communication.

Yes, I could create and deliver training both internally and externally. Yes, yes, yes was my answer to every question! Additionally, we were working on an offering that would provide customers access to information through their computers, connecting subscribers with helpful and up-to-the-minute information. Over the years, I've jokingly attributed the invention of the internet not to former Vice President Al Gore, but to Linda Waddell, the brilliant mind behind this new concept within our company. When she explained it to me, my excitement soared. However, I had limited experience with computers since my graduate school days when we still used Fortran cards. Nonetheless, it all sounded fantastic. Little did I know how challenging it would be.

My role involved assisting in the development of the sales and marketing strategy for this innovative concept. I would train our staff on email and try to persuade companies to embrace this new method of communication. Unfortunately, the initial responses I received were often along the lines of: "Great idea, but I'll wait and see," or "Get a couple of big companies to commit to using email and then come back and see me," or "Come back in six months." It's amusing to look back on it now.

Email is considered essential for most organizations, but it wasn't an easy sell in the beginning. A second challenge was figuring out how to convince customers to purchase information online such as weather, sports, and other helpful up to the minute information on their cell phones.

It's funny when we think about all the advances that have taken place since then. This was also around the time that portable computers were invented.

The team Linda compiled was amazing. They were all super-smart, diligent in attaining knowledge, and expert in the areas for which they were responsible. It was truly an amazing opportunity to work with such brilliant people. I was the only African American and Asian within the department. Linda was one of the most progressive bosses I've ever worked for, so it was not a race issue. Rather she compiled a group of skilled and knowledgeable people with specific areas of expertise. Everyone worked hard. It was the most amazing grouping of personalities. We all worked in a former company garage and so were sort of isolated in our lab to create our magic. Each personality had an impact on my life.

As you would imagine that fear of not belonging, not

measuring up, again surfaced its ugly head. I wasn't very proficient at using the computer, nor any of the software packages or programs that our young folks don't even think twice about today. I spent many evenings and weekends in the office or at home figuring out what I needed to know. I asked many questions and put in incredible hours to bring myself up to speed. But I was fighting major insecurities as well. I was "swanning" like a champ though under that water, those webbed feet told a different story!

The head of the department, down to the most junior person were all very supportive. My boss at that time, Anne D. had more confidence in me than I had in myself. It was one of the best environments professionally and personally that a person of my tender age could have been exposed that early in my work career.

I have taken the spirit of the amazing Linda Waddell who had more of an impact on my life than she will ever know, as well as all those strong men and women who helped me to excel. They were truly my work family. During that period, I also got married, had children, and finally got my master's degree in hand. I have fond memories of all those occasions where they celebrated me and my accomplishments. Everyone should be so lucky to work in that type of environment.

My subsequent environments were all great. I can't think of one environment where I was unhappy. My changing jobs and companies had more to do with my need for change and to keep moving forward. Fortunately, I've only experienced one environment toward the end of my corporate career when I fully understood when folks say that people don't leave companies, they leave bosses.

I could handle the work, and I could handle the people and politics around me, but I didn't and never will work well with leaders who rule with a vinegar, rather than sugar approach. The universe will always let you know when it's time to take the next step.

Professionally, I amassed an incredible amount of experience and growth working within that group, and within the company. My personal life was proceeding as it should have for a twenty-something young woman with a great career and a bright future.

Professionally, I felt confident I was navigating as expected, learning a lot, but I seemed to have a pretty grasp of what I needed to do to be successful. Besides the occasional bouts with imposter syndrome, I felt strong, steady and optimistic. I was also a hard worker and committed to doing things "the right way."

I'd say that my love life in my younger days was normal as well. Not to be cliche, but I am a hopeless romantic. I love that feeling of falling in love and being in love. I've only had a handful (literally) of serious boyfriends in my life. I had one high school boyfriend, one in undergrad, one in graduate school, and two that would eventually become my husbands. I've experienced the feeling of falling in love and being in love less than a handful of times. Besides the boyfriends, I had my share of dating stories.

Remember, I had trust issues dating back to kindergarten and coming home to my padlocked house. As a result, it would be many years into my adulthood before I could learn to fully trust anyone.

I dated some doozies. Despite how I appeared on the outside, I wasn't that confident in myself when it came to relationships, and I certainly had my share of expectations, as well as a boatload of baggage.

There was the one, "Rod" who had issues with infidelity

and exploited my low self-esteem, convincing me that I would never find anyone better than him. I loved him but ignored the obvious signs. He was a nice guy. He cooked, was neat, was a gentleman who treated me well, but also cheated on me. He'd been raised in a male-dominated family where most of the uncles had multiple relationships and more than one set of children by different women. He looked up to them but swore he was different. He ended up not being that different, and the universe told me in no uncertain terms that this was not the one. I'm not blaming him. Where I was in my life, I didn't believe I could do any better.

In one instance, I had just adopted a new rescue kitten from a shelter after I saw a mouse in my apartment. I am obsessed with keeping a clean house because of my deep fear of bugs and mice. I left the shelter and headed straight to this dude's house to introduce him to my new baby. I thought I'd surprise him, but I was the one who got the surprise. I spotted his brand-new shiny sports car a few cars ahead of me and followed him. Once he spotted me behind him, he pulled over and quickly jumped out of this car.

I thought I saw a little pea-shaped head in the passenger side of the car. He quickly ran to the driver's side of my car, looking quite nervous. I told him I was on my way to his house to introduce him to my new cat.

I then got out of my car and walked to the passenger side of his car and this voluptuous woman with a sexy animal print blouse looked up sheepishly at me. He introduced her as someone from his Bible Study group that he was giving a ride home. I just snickered at that and said "Yeah, right." walked back to my car and got in. I should have been upset, right? But seeing him in a compromising position only made me laugh. Later that evening, I asked myself how I could have found it funny. I should have been devastated, right? I knew it was time to close that chapter of my life. Shortly thereafter, we ended up parting on good terms and remained friends.

Then there was "Justin" whose family was afraid of the little Buddhist girl. He and I came from two different spiritual worlds, and his family enjoyed what I can only refer to as some type of religious superiority, and constantly judged me because I was an actively practicing Buddhist. They all claimed to be devout Christians, though there were some displays of clear religious hypocrisy and a lot of intolerance toward me.

I spent and enjoyed many holiday dinners with his family who were nice-enough people. But I didn't look forward to the long, drawn-out post-dinner conversations questioning the validity of my religion. They would sometimes go on for hours, with the boyfriend unfortunately not feeling comfortable defending me, or simply asking them to stand down.

The upside was that this expected questioning kept me on my toes. I had to make sure I was prepared and well-versed to handle their questions. I would confidently answer their questions without debating. I'd share quotes and historical facts and do my best to provide explanations and clarifications.

Never once did I question their beliefs, or the fact that some of them displayed what I sometimes perceived as behavior inconsistent with their beliefs they shared with me. I didn't blame them. They were protecting their beliefs and were concerned for their relative.

I am a lifetime a member of my sorority and belong to several organizations that have roots in Christianity. I was married by Baptist ministers and have been in many Black churches in Philadelphia in support of friends and family at weddings, dedications, funerals, and just to hear sermons.

Truthfully, there are more similarities among all religions than there are differences. For me, the important thing is that we hold ourselves accountable to something greater than ourselves. We all know the difference between right and wrong and understand that what we put out, we get back: good, bad, or other.

I am the only Buddhist friend of many of my Christian friends. I am extremely grateful for the tolerance and acceptance of so many of my friends. I couldn't imagine a future that required me to justify my religion after virtually every big family meal for the rest of my life. I later learned his story was that he broke up with me because he couldn't handle my religion. If that was his truth, I was okay with his narrative.

Then there was the consistently irresponsible one. Jared had been on thin ice for a while. My teenage niece was visiting from Virginia, and on the day before I was scheduled to take her back home, he and I agreed to take her to an amusement park. I don't like to get on the scary rides, so we agreed ahead of time that the two of them would go on the daredevil rides together. The morning of the trip came, and I couldn't reach him by phone. My niece and I got dressed and drove over to his house to pick him up. When we arrived, I left her in the car out front, thinking this would only take a few minutes to get him. I went upstairs to his room and found him still in bed, sprawled out, barely moving. I asked him why he wasn't ready to go to the amusement park. He said he didn't feel good. I could smell the alcohol coming through his pores. He was so hung over he could barely move. Mind you, this is after several rough weeks where I'd been questioning where our relationship was going. The signs were all there. Looking back, I don't even blame him. I blame myself for not realizing my worth and lacking the courage to walk away sooner.

This last-minute change of plans was also not uncharacteristic of some of the things he had done before. I can't recall what I said, but I'm sure it wasn't anything polite. He then said in a low and even voice: "Shut up and get out."

Whattt?

I won't bore you with the details except to say that within a few minutes, I'd reached that point at which I said the final "ENOUGH." His roommate "Stanley" heard the commotion and came up and knocked on his door. He told me he was coming in.

I told him that it wasn't a good idea for him to try to come in. He opted to stay on the other side of the door. Smart dude.

It took me a few minutes to regain my composure and once calm, I realized it was not worth the energy to keep trying to salvage whatever this was.

Tears sprang to my eyes because I knew this was the final, FINAL breakup. Then that hard, belly wrenching cry started. I then remembered that my niece was in the car waiting for me. I turned around and walked down the stairs, took some deep breaths, wiped my tears as best I could with my sleeves, took a few more deep breaths, put on my sunglasses, and got back in the car.

I said, in my best high-pitched, fake, overly happy voice, "Well, it looks like it's just going to be me and you."

"Okay," She replied. She didn't ask any questions, nor did I volunteer any additional information. I then proceeded to drive my niece to the amusement park. I was amazed at how quickly I was able to pull myself together, and that physical release made me feel better.

My adrenaline was still racing as I got on the road. I'm sure I was speeding when a few miles into the trip, I looked back and saw the flashing lights of a police cruiser behind me.

My first thought:
"Oh shucks, I'm going to get a speeding ticket."

My second thought: "Did he call the police on me for the ruckus I caused? Was I that bad?"

But when I saw the officer, "Trevor," whom I recognized get out of the car, panic started setting in. It was a mutual friend of mine and the soon-to-be ex-boyfriend.

Fortunately, we didn't have to stay in our vehicles when we got stopped back then. I got out of the car, as my niece didn't need to know what was going on.

He ran up to me and gave me a big hug. Whew! I realized that he hadn't yet heard that I created a commotion at his boy's house. He'd recognized my car and was just stopping me to say hi. We chatted for a few minutes, and I got back in the car.

I would have loved to have been a fly on the wall when he later mentioned to my now ex that he saw me on the road that day. I'm certain the roommate couldn't resist telling the officer/friend about the ruckus the little crazy Japanese girl caused that morning. I'm still chuckling about it.

My niece and I ended up having an awesome time at the theme park. I closed my eyes through all the scary rides and was happy at the end of the day to have survived. We had a great day, and an uneventful ride home.

That following morning, I picked up my mom before getting on the road to drive my niece back to Virginia. Mom was great company and a welcome distraction on the ride back home. The long drive was also helpful in clearing my head. Mom had no idea what was going on in the background, and I preferred it that way. I didn't want her giving me the "you're about to let another good man go, now you won't ever get married" speech.

By the time I got back home, I knew what I needed to do. If I could allow myself to get that emotional and expend that type of negative energy on someone as I had done the day before, we did not belong together. The next day I called him and notified him that this time it was for good. He simply said "Okay." Fortunately, none of those guys I described ended up becoming a husband of mine.

And yes, of course there were some princes.

The next one was prince potential — a home grown crazy-smart dude who knew everyone, and everyone knew him. Called me unworldly on our first date. He was surprised we hadn't met earlier.

I wasn't insulted. This "unworldliness" worked to my benefit at times. It brings to mind the Japanese quote I mentioned earlier: "Shiranu ga hotoke," meaning "Ignorance is bliss."

Because I grew up in what he labeled "geographically undesirable" neighborhoods, I wasn't exposed to many of the Old Philadelphia, Old Guard Black people. The benefit of that? When I would accompany my guy to parties, I knew virtually no one, and not many people knew me.

At these parties, it wasn't unusual for me to hang around him and the guys. I was more comfortable with them. We went to one such party in the neighborhood in which he grew up, and the attendees seemed to all know one another. I was a total outsider, and pretty much hung with him and his friends. I think I met a couple of women. It wasn't until later that evening after we left the party that he told me who some of the people were. Because I didn't know who was whom, I felt no pressure to act any differently than normal. I "appreciated" my ignorance.

This dude "Maxwell" came along and swept me off my feet. He was movie star handsome, smart, charming, and funny. He was also well- loved and respected. This was the ideal combination for me. He lived in the DMV. It could be a fun and casual thing, right? I wasn't interested in a long-distance relationship. We hit it off immediately, and before I knew it, I found myself falling into a deeper level of love than I had ever before experienced. This one would end up being the right one. He was deep, knowledgeable, and had a great sense of humor. His intelligence scared me. But he also made me feel loved, valued, and for the first time in my life, safe.

After our first date, he asked me, "Why didn't you tell me you grew up in the projects?" Confused, I responded, "What projects?" He had taken me to a party and introduced me to his best friend Whitney, whom I recognized from my childhood. Whitney had lived in the newly built development near my apartment with the fancy name. He said, "Whit told me you lived in the projects." I was perplexed and wondered aloud, "I didn't live in the projects. Wait, were they projects?"

If someone heard that response, they might think I was ashamed and hiding that detail. The truth was, I didn't know the apartments in which we lived were considered projects. No one had ever referred to them as such, so how would I have been familiar with that label? I was confused, and repeated the question out loud: "Were they projects?" They weren't projects. If they were, that was a pretty fancy name for projects.

The following week, I drove back to that neighborhood, looked around, and chuckled to myself: "Yeah, I lived in the projects." From that day on, I embraced my upbringing in the projects as a badge of honor. Hey, I now had an addition to my own "poor girl makes good" story.

Yes, when he and I met, I was a clueless, rough around the edges girl from the 'hood. Of course, one of the first things we do when we see potential in someone is conduct our research, right? That's what he did.

This was another occasion when the poor grades I earned in my first year of high school came back to haunt me, when he asked one of my high school classmates about me. This friend of his knew about my grades, as he was part of the student council that vetted candidates and warned him, "She's a dumb party chick. Have fun with her, but don't get serious."

I shared with him the mistakes I made in my freshman year of high school. I admitted that I was a party chick (well I might have exaggerated on that because that part sounded cool), but not a dumb one.

I encouraged him to get to know me and judge for himself. I was at that point where I wasn't wasting my energy trying to prove anything otherwise. I'd already spent too much of my youth trying to prove I wasn't a cute but dumb chick. I'm amazed at the amount of maneuvering I had done up to that point to prove myself and try to fit in. I was beyond that point.

Despite the warning, things continued to progress between me and my guy and we decided to move in together. It made perfect sense for numerous reasons, and we both believed that marriage was in our future. At that time, all three of my siblings were already married with children. I had been getting pressure from Mom about when we would get married. I had already been engaged twice before, so the idea of my still being unmarried concerned her. I was a smart, successful professional with a pretty awesome life, a couple of dollars in my pocket, and a promising future. I didn't share Mom's concern.

But I was afraid to tell my mom or any of my siblings that he and I had moved in together. We took extreme measures such as getting separate phone lines, and I think one of us got a post office box. I don't recall inviting my siblings over, as I feared they'd tell my parents. Such deception. A grown woman going to such great lengths to keep this from her mother. I'm sure some of my fellow Blasians can relate. I'm pretty sure my mom never knew we were living together.

He was an amazing man and it was one of the greatest romances of my life. He was a keeper for sure. I wish I could say more about him. Those were some of my dating and great romance stories.

Meanwhile, professionally, I was in a really great place. Believe it or not, the biggest challenges I faced were related to my need to be taken seriously. I worked hard at looking the part so I would be taken seriously. I also looked younger than I was at twenty-five-ish, and I wore conservative suits with corny bowties, pulled my hair into a bun and sometimes wore glasses to look older (and smarter). I made major fashion choices to solidify my professional look.

About ten years into my career, I recall making a huge presentation wearing a two-piece skirt suit and found the department head staring at my legs. Being the extremist I was sometimes accused of being, I started wearing pants, pantsuits, and maxi skirts. Because of my height, my short torso, and my long legs, the maxi skirts were not an attractive look at all. But I went with them.

Beauty:
Blessing or Curse?

Delicately navigating this topic, I want to address the taboo surrounding women others describe as beautiful, discussing beauty. Now that I have reached a more advanced age, I have come to terms with the fading of my looks and have permitted myself to embrace aging gracefully. It is from this standpoint that I feel comfortable discussing the dichotomy of beauty—an enigma that can be both a gift and a curse. I vividly remember my mentor, Linda Waddell, the brilliant member of Mensa who had a sign in her office that read, "I know I'm brilliant, tell me I'm beautiful."

I admit how deeply I longed for a sign proclaiming, "Don't tell me I'm beautiful, tell me I'm brilliant," without sounding full of myself.

Stereotypes abound when it comes to attractive women, and unfortunately, many of them are not positive. There is an automatic assumption that if you possess beauty, you must lack intelligence. Or you're "crazy." Heck, we all have our share of "crazy"-whatever that means.

Moreover, people often assume that attractive women are self-absorbed and unfriendly. Early on, I discovered that being kind and approachable, especially to attractive women, was a welcome surprise for those around me. If given the choice between intelligence and physical beauty, I think I would choose the former.

Those close to me understand how defensive I get when I perceive others questioning my intelligence. I must emphasize that any beauty I have been "blessed with" is not a result of my own efforts. I am simply grateful to have inherited great genes from my Asian and African American parents. And I've worked hard at preserving the gifts I inherited. Growing up, I was what some would call a "tomboy" (if we can still use that term). However, my mother had a strong desire to dress me up and make me look like a little doll.

I will admit that dressing up made me feel good about myself, and I won't deny my enjoyment of the privileges that came with it. Enjoying free entry into parties, VIP access, receiving leniency from traffic violations, and getting extra driving school hours without cost—it was an undeniable benefit.

But, because beauty is often erroneously associated with a lack of intelligence, I frequently encountered dismissive attitudes that undermined my intellectual capabilities. To be honest, I sometimes played into those assumptions to disarm people. Being underestimated also had its advantages.

However, there came a point when I took offense at any insinuation that I lacked intelligence. I would expend unnecessary energy in many attempts to prove just how smart I was.

The other thing that sets me off is when I am made to feel I am somehow responsible for unwanted attention or advances made toward me. Though I have always been friendly, I've also been careful to avoid sending mixed messages, in both my personal and professional life.

This reaction was triggered by an event very early in my life when I was the victim of unsolicited inappropriate, behavior in which I was blamed for encouraging it. As a result, I've been very intentional about avoiding situations that could be perceived as my "bringing this on myself."

However, on one occasion during this period, a significant event occurred that shook my sense of security. I didn't pursue further action the way I should have.

One evening, I was startled by loud noises outside of my apartment building. Peering out my apartment window, I was horrified to see two cars engulfed in flames. I looked closer and realized that one of the burning cars was mine! I called the fire department, who arrived promptly and extinguished the fires. The police initiated a brief investigation. My car was totaled. A few days later, a detective contacted me, informing me that someone set my car on fire, and it spread to the vehicle behind mine when the flames ignited the "bra" on the front of that car.

Shockingly, the detective began aggressively interrogating me over the phone. Was there a jealous husband, an ex, or anyone I had recently rejected seeking revenge? At the time, I was exclusively seeing one man. While I had an admirer who lived in my building and a few men who had asked me out over the two years I'd lived in that apartment complex, I couldn't imagine any of them doing anything like this. The detective insisted on meeting face to face, but based on his accusatory line of questioning, I decided it was not in my best interest. He would surely blame the victim. Unsurprisingly, I never heard from him again, and the case remained unsolved. However, this incident left me feeling excessively cautious, constantly watching my back. My sense of safety was shattered, prompting me to move away from that neighborhood as soon as the opportunity arose. I've shared that story and its aftermath with very few people because I knew the assumption was likely that I'd somehow brought it on myself.

The concept of beauty carries with it a complex set of experiences. It can be both a gift and a curse, entangled in societal stereotypes and expectations. As I reflect on my journey, I have learned to embrace my intelligence while acknowledging the transient nature of physical appearance. In the meantime, let people underestimate me.

I ended up replacing the car, but it took me a long time to regain some sense of security. But life went on.

That next year was pivotal. In 1989, the book "Joy Luck Club" had been released. Although it was primarily a work of fiction, I'm pretty sure that many who grew up with Asian parents and moms specifically, found themselves both nodding and shaking their heads throughout the various storylines. It was the first time I realized that so many of us Asian Americans shared similar stories. I became curious about my Japanese family and resolved to somehow connect with them.

The following year, I took my first trip to Japan. I accomplished two major things on this trip. I participated in my first-ever Buddhist pilgrimage to the temples in Japan, and I also met my mother's family, from whom she had been separated for over three decades. Upon meeting my aunts, I was immediately struck by the uncanny resemblance they bore to my mother.

What struck me even more was the similarity in their mannerisms. Their movements, speech, and way they carried themselves were so like Mom's. Their gestures and expressions gave me a sense of familiarity like I'd known them for my entire life. Despite my limited knowledge of the Japanese language and their limited command of English, we understood one another far more than anyone would expect.

I tried to memorize every interaction, every shared moment, which all gave me "mini-glimpses" into the interesting tapestry of my family's history. Though brief, my time with them not only allowed me to create this bond with my extended family but I also established an indescribable connection to my roots on a profoundly personal level. We took lots of pictures and communicated pretty well despite the language barrier. They fondly called me their "eiga no suta" (movie star).

The time spent with my mother's family in Japan gifted me with more than just cherished memories. It gave me a profound sense of belonging and a deeper appreciation for the uniqueness of my diverse blend.

It taught me that despite the vast differences that exist in the world, the ties that bind us as a family and as human beings are unbreakable, resilient, and capable of transcending barriers, regardless of the briefness of the time we were together.

The visit also gave me a more profound understanding and appreciation of Mom. She and I were always very close. Before starting my own family, I spent a significant amount of time with her. I took her on many personal and business trips with me. She and I had regular dates where I took her out to eat, shop, and chat about nearly anything. I valued the time we spent together, and her joy at experiencing new things filled me with happiness.

I still filled the role of handling most of her business, taxes, doctor's appointments, and other personal things. Though I felt Mom was extra tough on me, I prided myself on being a dutiful daughter, and I was proud to say that I "spoiled" my mom.

In 1993, I went to see the movie inspired by the book The Joy Luck Club and found myself shedding cathartic tears. It prompted me to reflect on the decisions my mother made in coming to this country, and her many sacrifices she'd made. I felt immense gratitude toward her. I imagine that the hardest thing a young mother can do is to leave her family. I can't even begin to fathom having to leave my mom and move halfway across the world as she had done with my dad.

After watching the movie, I also felt seen and heard for the first time, in a different way. I wondered, and still do, why our stories haven't been shared more widely.

Up to that point, very few major motion pictures had been released depicting the Asian-American experience.

Having friends who are Asian and those who share my same biracial makeup is truly great. I can recall conversations we all had after we'd read the book, and again after we saw the movie. As we laughed together, we marveled at the misperceptions surrounding our Asian mothers, whom the world often labels as reserved, unassertive, and even submissive. We all knew that our moms defied those stereotypes!

I appreciate that today, much more Japanese culture is available. I make it a point to seek out documentaries, movies and even anime that share the Japanese experience.

My life continued to expand. Married a few years by now, life was going great. I was making connections, navigating major moves, and gaining exposure to different circles. The poor little swan from the projects was expanding her wings. I was experiencing so many wonderful changes. Throughout it all, I maintained a grateful heart and always vowed to remain humble no matter what. I shared what I had with others. Some told me (and still say) that I was generous to a fault. I say, "There is no such thing." I've had so many people help me, and I take pleasure in helping others.

But as my lifestyle expanded, some key relationships changed, as well as how some people perceived me. Simple words and phrases can carry immense weight. I started hearing "You've changed." It was not spoken positively, but more like an accusation. I hated hearing those words and would immediately jump on the defensive. Or I'd do some unproductive things to convince folks that I hadn't changed.

It got to the point where hearing those words started to fill me with dread, instantly triggering anxiety. I grew tired of hearing it, especially from the same few people. Yes, my circumstances had changed, but I believed I was fundamentally the same person at my core.

It was at this point that I began to realize that we should all be changing as we grow. If I am the same person I was in my youth, naïve, unworldly, and clueless—then how much progress have I made? How has my progress benefited those around me?

It dawned on me that there were people who would never acknowledge nor remember the many ways my progress benefited them. So, I decided to distance myself from said people. Luckily, the list was very, very short. I have always been and continue to be confident in my own values and belief system. Another triggering phrase was, "You've become a snob."

Oh my Gosh, I can't tell you how quickly that accusation would instantly propel me into defense mode. How it was said turned it into a weapon that would immediately put me on guard. This went on for years until my then-husband who'd witnessed this interaction numerous times, gave me the best advice: "Embrace it. You've worked hard for what you have. Let them have their definition. If being a snob means striving for success and doing the best for yourself and your family and for those whom you care, then own it." What great advice! From that point on, I accepted his definition as my own. It was liberating to take away the power those simple words held over me.

For years, some folks labeled me as "too busy." That was another label used to refer to me in a negative way that I'd never been able to shake. The truth? We invest our time with people and things that give us something back. That something could be calm, peace, acceptance, laughter, or a million other things. I chose to distance myself from those whom I felt constantly judged me.

A second truth? I was really busy. I was now adjusting to marriage, running a home together, building a life as a couple, becoming a mother, working full-time, engaging in volunteer activities, and balancing the guilt associated with trying to do it all.

Besides, relationships are two-way, and we both have equal ability to pick up the phone. You want to chat? You can always call me and not wait for me to call.

But here's the biggest thing: I choose not to let those words define me. Even today, I won't allow someone else's misguided perception of me to shape who I am. Instead, I'll continue to focus on rising above any negativity. It's not about proving anyone wrong or seeking validation. No, it's about staying true to myself and refusing to let anything poison my spirit. You can have your "truth" about me.

As I mentioned, change is a natural part of life. People grow, evolve, and sometimes outgrow certain relationships. If you sense a shift in my interactions with you, it's not out of spite or a desire to be vindictive. It's simply a reflection of the changes that have occurred within me. Life has a way of teaching us valuable lessons, and sometimes those lessons necessitate a re-evaluation of the company we keep.

In the end, it's important to remember that our worth is not determined by the labels others place upon us. We are not defined by the words of those who choose to judge or criticize. Rather, we define ourselves through our actions, integrity, and the way we navigate the world with authenticity and kindness.

As I've entered different phases of my life, I've naturally attracted those with whom I share commonalities. By commonalities, I mean lifestyle, profession, values, and similar circumstances. I had more in common with my friends who were going through the same life changes as me including home life, children, balancing work, and self-care.

It was during this time in my life that I met an amazing young woman, Tina, who would eventually become my best friend. She's a few years younger than me, bright, beautiful, intelligent, and has a genuine, amazing spirit. I instantly liked her. We met at a trade show when she had just started working for the company for whom I worked. Strangely enough, my first piece of advice to her was to make sure she prioritized paying herself first and asked if she participated in the company's 401k program, highlighting that the match was essentially free money. I know, it was an unusual conversation for a first encounter. I recall it, but I don't think she does.

My crew and I ran into Tina and her crew again at an industry conference for Black professionals in Atlantic City a little less than a year later. Our respective crews bonded when we decided to go to a chain restaurant, just before news broke out about their organization's systematic provision of poor service to African Americans. Despite being overdressed in formal attire, we experienced the same mistreatment. We connected over the shared injustice we faced and ended up all going to a diner together. I remain good friends with nearly all of them today. Tina's presence and impact on my life would grow to a point where I can't imagine my life before we met. There have been countless key moments in history that we've experienced together. Her friendship is truly a gift to me, and I am grateful for her.

Motherhood:
A Life Changer

And then I experienced motherhood. Parenting for me, has been a multifaceted journey that began long before I gave birth. It's not uncommon for individuals to develop and practice their parenting skills even before having children of their own. The role I played in caring for my mom gave me confidence that I'd be okay as a parent of my own children.

Additionally, my nephew and niece, Steven and Shardae, played significant roles in my life, as they spent a considerable amount of time with me, particularly before I had my own children. Through my experiences with them, I had the opportunity to embrace the joys and challenges of nurturing and guiding young minds. Investing time and energy into their growth brought me profound fulfillment. I loved and adored them as if they were mine.

My family and I shared many holidays with Steven and Shardae and took them on trips. This spoke volumes about the special bond and trust I shared with their mother, who generously allowed me to be a part of their lives. Their dad, my brother, lived in a different state.

The memories of these joyous occasions are deeply ingrained in my heart. Both children were well-behaved, another testament to the positive influence of their mom and dad on them. I loved taking them to my workplace when we opened our offices to families during holidays.

Despite the passage of time and the changing dynamics of life, my nephew Steven and I have managed to maintain a strong and close relationship. Parenthood should not be solely defined by biological relationships but rather by the love, guidance, and support one provides to young individuals as they grow and develop. And I received so much love and joy from them.

When I gave birth to my first child, Kendall, my entire outlook on life changed. In that moment, as I looked into his beautiful big brown innocent eyes, I understood that my heart was no longer mine. It had been irrevocably claimed by this tiny being who was a part of me.

Love surged through my veins, and if I'm honest, a healthy dose of fear. I grasped the enormity of this lifelong voyage of nurturing, protecting, and guiding this precious soul.

I would again experience this unique dose of magic a little less than two years later when I discovered I was again pregnant with yet another baby boy. I was overjoyed.

But during this pregnancy, I also lost my beloved paternal grandmother. It was a bittersweet period of my life. My grandmother and I had a very special relationship that I cherished. In addition to all the memories I shared growing up, Mom never stopped showing me how much she loved me, and how proud she was of me. The entire time I was in college, both undergrad and graduate school, Mom sent me checks every month. Some months she sent ten dollars, sometimes fifteen, and for my birth month, a whopping twenty-five dollars. She never missed a month. Into adulthood, I maintained a close relationship with her. One of my favorite annual rituals that began after I completed college and continued until she passed at the age of seventy-eight, was spending an entire day with her in early December. We spent the time prepping for Christmas. I would wrap all of her Christmas gifts she bought for everyone while she cooked me dinner. We would then eat together.

Mom had also taught me to cook soul food when I was in my twenties. She told me if I knew how to cook, I could always get and keep a man. I'm not sure if that was any motivation for me but I am a pretty good cook today.

Mom taught me how to thoroughly clean fresh collard greens. She would make me count the number of times I washed and rinsed them. She also taught me to make sweet potato pies, and quiche. Later, when the doctors advised her that she had to eat more heart-healthy food, she introduced me to more healthy recipes. They didn't taste as good but helped me to understand that all food need not taste great if it offered other benefits. I have so many fond memories of my grandmother and was deeply grateful for her unconditional love. I mourned the fact that my second son would never meet this wonderful woman who'd meant so much to me.

My children were, and remain, everything to me. I don't have to mention how much I loved and still love motherhood and being a "bonus" mother and grandmother as well.

I make no apologies for the unwavering love and protection I shower upon them, or for how I respond, even today, to those who dare mistreat our beloved children.

But it goes beyond the simple act of parenting. My children were, and still are, the mirrors through which I discovered my strengths and weaknesses. I am grateful for the privilege of being their mother. In the embrace of motherhood, I found a different purpose, joy, and a love that knows no limits. I must acknowledge that I've made my share of mistakes along the journey of raising my boys to whom I gave birth. One thing they never have to question is my unrelenting love and concern for them.

I must also mention that I am unyielding when it comes to defending my loved ones from harm. At young ages, their vulnerability activated a primal ferocity within me, and I have countless stories about my fierce "Mama Bear" instinct. For fear of embarrassing them more than I have in their lives thus far, I won't get into too many details here.

There was one incident I know will stick with them and me, even if we all live to be a hundred. It was a time when my Brendan was on the soccer field with his shoelace untied. There was a short break in the game, so I dashed onto the field to tie it for him. Of course, the whistle blew for the game to restart before I'd finished. It was definitely not my finest moment as a mom, and I promise it happened only once!

Where there were lessons to be learned and I could make them "teachable moments," I did try to have discussions with my sons.

I went to pick Kendall up from a summer arts camp one day. He may have been five or six at the time. He saw me and started to come up to me while I was signing him out. When I'd finished, I looked around for him, but he'd suddenly disappeared. It took me a few minutes to find him, and when I did, I asked him where he'd gone. It was clear he was upset and didn't want to talk about it, so I didn't press him.

I waited until we got in the car and drove off to ask him again. He told me that the mother of one of his fellow campmates (a little girl whom I think he liked) told him to come with her. I asked: "But why didn't you tell me you were walking away?"

He said: "I had to go with her because she was a police officer. She told me to stop talking to her daughter."

"WHAT?"!!

SCREEEEECH! I hit the brakes a little harder than I intended.

"Mom, don't," he pleaded.

I sighed and replied, "Babe, I have no choice."

A few seconds later, my huge SUV was in serious U-turn mode. I was also trying to breathe, struggling to keep calm for my son's sake. This kid's mom, a police officer in uniform, used her position to intimidate a child. Not just any child. My child.

By the time we got back to the camp, the mother and her child were gone. I communicated my concern about the obvious abuse of power to the camp's director. The camp would not, surely could not, give me her or the child's name. It was my son's last week at that camp, but he had two more days to go. In those last two days, I arrived early to drop him off and pick him up, looking for a uniformed policewoman. If she came those last two days, she was not in uniform. I didn't want to put my son in the middle, so I remained as discrete as I could.

I used this as a teachable moment, sharing the "bad sides" of anyone misusing their power. Lesson to my son: Just because they have a uniform doesn't give them the right to intimidate others.

I was likely fortunate that they were gone when we came back. But after I calmed down, I wanted the opportunity to talk to her, mother to mother, and ask her:

"What kind of message are you conveying to your daughter?" How would you feel if someone abused their power to intimidate your child?

I definitely had my issues with anger as a young and

protective mom. No one talked about emotional intelligence. In looking back, I was sorely lacking emotional intelligence when I was younger. As a new mom, if I had any semblance of self-awareness or awareness of others, I would have protected myself and others from so many avoidable mistakes.

My son liked a little girl who attended the same day care as he. He talked about her every day. He asked me to ask her parents (whom we'd met) if the little girl could come over to our house for a playdate. I wrote a nice little note to her parents and asked if we could arrange a playdate between their daughter and our son. I got no response. About a week later, this same son and I were sitting together one evening, and he seemed a little sad. I asked him if he wanted to talk about it. He reluctantly told me that the little girl was having a birthday party, and he hadn't been invited.

Being the overly protective Mom I was, I immediately got annoyed, though I didn't show it. "How dare they treat my perfect little handsome, sensitive, smart child like this?" "That's okay," I replied. "We won't invite her to your birthday party." He looked up at me, puzzled, and said,

"But I want her to come."

I was taken aback, as I realized what had just taken place. How it starts, where we take these children's innocent thoughts and subtly and not so subtly teach them our "life lessons."

What I, his mom had conveyed to him is that we treat others the same way they treat us. If they reject us, we, in turn, reject them. That only matters if you matter to the other person. When you exact revenge on someone and you don't even register on their "matter" list, there is no win, morally or otherwise. As he genuinely liked her and wanted to be around her, I gave him the wrong response.

I learned a profound lesson from my young son that day. I

look back on that now, and just as I wanted to ask the woman police officer what kind of message she was sending to her daughter? I should have asked myself, "What kind of message am I sending to my son?"

I ended up inviting the little girl to his party, though she didn't come. That was her loss. It was a great party. My son moved on pretty quickly.

These are just a couple of my many "Mommy stories," most of which I don't regret—except perhaps the tying the shoelace on the soccer field. It all came from a place of love.

While my sons may have cringed at my "helicoptering" back then, I hope as they have matured that they have come to understand the intention behind it.

There were also battles over things for which I chose to fight and some I opted to ignore. One recurring battle was with table manners, which has taken up far more time and energy across generations in my family than necessary. My mom instilled in us the importance of having good table manners. While my parents taught us many valuable lessons, some of them I decided to question, rethink, and redefine once I became a mother. During my ultra-busy years balancing career and personal life, I aspired to maximize the valuable and sometimes scarce time I had with my children. I'd see my mom in me as I nagged them about using the right utensils, not using their fingers to eat, not speaking with their mouth full.

I also realized that if I spent the entire time nagging them about things they'd eventually learn, I'd take the fun out of dinners out, and other outings together. I decided their table manners were not worth the fight at that time and took deep breaths when I wanted to nag them. A lot of times I was successful, though sometimes I wasn't and gave into my urge to nag. Fortunately, my sons have pretty good table manners at the right times. The other times? I don't give a hoot.

Balancing marriage, a demanding career and two children was challenging for me. I was in my twelfth year at a great company, in a management role that suited me well when I first returned to work after my youngest was born. It was not super demanding, so I could work hours that enabled me to have mealtime with my family, and not be on e-mail throughout the nights and weekends. I had, from the time the children were born, an amazing support network between our family members and a very large family who embraced us as part of their family.

I think I was in my safe "Mommy Track" job for about six months when I began looking for a new role, and shortly thereafter received an offer from PECO Energy. It was a great next step. I recall talking to my then mother-in-law, who asked me: "Are you sure about leaving your good job?" Back in our parents' day, people stayed with the same company for their entire careers. I loved working for my company, I just didn't see how I could get off the "Mommy Track" in the timeframe I wanted.

Joining PECO exposed me to a fantastic opportunity. They gave me an incredible executive coach and invested in me from the first day. The president and the entire leadership of our group were phenomenal. My boss was great, taught me a lot, and helped me grow. I was in a new and developing area that would eventually form an unregulated arm of the company. The learning curve was steep, and the role required more travel than I expected, but I quickly grew to love the job, the people, and the company. I felt challenged, I was doing meaningful work, and contributing to the department's bottom line.

There were also challenges that in retrospect, I could have handled differently. My travel quickly increased as we began acquiring and merging companies, which increased my travel even more. Life was busy balancing work, home, and looking after Mom, among other demands of my time.

As a working mom, I still tried to make as many of their school activities as I could. I made it a point to be there for the really important stuff. But the truth was, I missed some of the ordinary but still important things like picking them up from school and taking them to practice, among others.

On top of all of that, my dad had a heart attack. I was on my way to Atlanta for a business conference when Mom Sandy called to inform me. I dropped everything and rushed to his side. It was the first time I recall ever seeing my father lying in a hospital bed. This happened about a year after his retirement and subsequent return to the Philly area to care for his stepmother, following his father's passing.

At that time, I worked out of offices in various locations, one of which was conveniently close to where he lived. Since his and Mom Sandy's return to Philly, we'd begun spending more time together.

It was the first time in decades that Daddy and I lived in the same area since I left for college. I developed a closer, different adult relationship with him, and with Mom Sandy, whom I grew to love as well. Daddy would come over to fix things at my house, I would visit them, and we talked on the phone frequently. Both he and Sandy loved my cooking, and I loved cooking for them.

I cherished having my dad actively involved in my life. His heart attack served as even more of a wake-up call. Fortunately, he survived the heart attack and recovered. Little did I know this would be the beginning of one of the most difficult ongoing challenges of my life - witnessing my father's health deteriorate year after year. I'm sad to admit that there were times when I would be so sad that I would avoid spending time with him. I also know I didn't always express my gratitude to Mom Sandy. She took amazing care of Daddy, and was the true, literal definition of "ride or die."

By then, I had been with the company for a couple of years when it made good on its announcement that it was ready to divest itself into a separate organization (as planned when I accepted the job). The company was required to provide every one of its employees in my department with formal offers to go with the new company they created. The alternative was that each of us could take a package offered to everyone, whether we were opting to go with the new company or not.

I was faced with one of the most difficult decisions of my life. After all, I would be leaving a job, without a job or any prospects. After praying for the best outcome, I agreed to play it safe, stay, and join the newly forming company. I had two weeks to change my mind, and I mulled over my decision the entire two weeks. I also continued to pray for a sign that I was making the best decision. I have always believed that if we are open to seeing the signs, the universe always has a way of communicating the best path.

On day fourteen, in the afternoon, I was working from my home office. I was on a conference call which was going well. Naturally, I was distracted, watching the clock tick. Then someone said something on the call that made me say to myself: "Don't be afraid."

Over the years, I've wracked my brain trying to recall what was said. But on the last day I could revoke my decision, with ten minutes to spare, I decided to leave the company. I faxed my final decision just before the 5:00 pm deadline on the last day after I revoked my waiver.

That night, I lay in bed, totally second-guessing my decision. I even contemplated getting to work extra early and taking my signed letter of resignation off the fax machine. I knew the president of my group wasn't happy with my decision and would have been okay with my taking it back.

I felt badly about the timing. I loved working for the company, and I enjoyed my job. The bigger issue for me was the amount of travel and being away from my family and aging parents. I was excited about the prospect of taking the package, which would allow me to take a professional break and buy myself and our family time to figure out the next step. I knew I didn't want to travel as much.

The day after I made the decision and submitted my two weeks' notice, the office was hosting a farewell lunch for those who decided to leave by the deadline two weeks before. It was at that luncheon that I informally told people that I too had decided to leave. I can remember one co-worker who asked me if I had another job. "No, it happened so quickly, I hadn't had a chance to truly think about that."

She gave me a serious look and said - "You are stepping out on faith." My heart started beating rapidly, and I felt actual fear upon hearing it spoken out loud. I put on that confident swan smile and coolly said "Yes, I am." I was suddenly terrified.

To make sure I was not leaving my company shorthanded, I stayed on as a consultant for another month. Over the final six weeks, I vacillated between excitement, terror, and every feeling in between.

For the first time besides my maternity leave breaks, I tried my hand at being a stay-at-home mom. I knew that with our lifestyle I couldn't do it forever. But I wanted to see what it would be like, as I also contemplated the next move that would benefit our family. To ensure the children wouldn't lose their spots at daycare, I adjusted their schedules to part-time. I began to work out, and we joined a nearby family pool, finding other ways to fill our time. Busy people always seem to find new things on which to focus when they take things off their plates, don't they? For me, it was the pursuit of the next accomplishment.

When school resumed in the fall for my oldest child, I tried to get more involved with the school. However, I struggled to adjust to the role of a PTO Mom. I held nothing but respect for them, but I didn't feel like I fit into what seemed like a mom's club, most of whom didn't look like me or my children. There's this funny friction that exists between Moms who work outside of the home and those who don't. It's an interesting dynamic. Each believes their way is the best, and understandably so. Our defense of our status is probably in part to reduce cognitive dissonance we may experience.

Excluding that short period of their lives (it only ended up being four months), I was a working mom. I'll bet my boys don't even remember that brief period. After only a month or so of enjoying my "break," I started looking for a new job. I was somewhat limited in my prospects as I needed to be nearby for my parents, especially my mom. Though both parents were aging, at least Daddy had Mom Sandy. My mom relied on me pretty heavily, two of my three siblings had left Philly when they graduated from high school and had lived in other states ever since. Because of that, relocating was never an option for me.

I appreciated the brief break but yearned to get back out in the working world.

"Comparison is The Thief of Joy."
-Theodore Roosevelt

For the most part, this quote holds true for me. But it requires conscious effort and mindfulness to break the habit of comparing ourselves to others. We face societal expectations that push us to aspire to reach whatever our next milestone represents. We fall into the trap of these predefined expectations, and it's challenging to put ourselves in other people's shoes and understand their struggles.

Those who appear to have picture-perfect lives often face just as many challenges as those of us who don't. I once heard someone say that people with less are often happier than those who seem to have it all, and it makes sense. People with fewer resources have hope and believe that acquiring certain things or earning more money will bring them happiness.

But those who have achieved their dreams and more, come to realize that material possessions and accomplishments are not the keys to happiness. I know many people who represent the perfect life on the surface: great jobs, marriages, perfect children, and a picture-perfect lifestyle. However, even they yearn for something more, questioning what comes next after achieving it all.

Counting our neighbor's blessings is a common habit. Of my many shortcomings, luckily, comparing myself to others is not one of them. I used to say that I'm grateful not to have the "comparison to others" gene.

I said it one day, and someone close to me responded, "It's

because you have everything you want." No, that was never true. But I am indeed satisfied and grateful for what I have. Jealousy and related emotions stem from comparison and yearning. Daily, I am surrounded by people whom I know are doing much better than I am in nearly every aspect of life, be it youth, intelligence, wealth, love, family, possessions, or professional success. Likewise, I am also surrounded by people who don't have the same fortune I do. I am content and at peace with where I am in my life. It took me a long time to reach this point, and the shift wasn't physical, but rather mental and spiritual.

As a kid, I loved the song by the Temptations called "Don't Let the Joneses Get You Down." Society and social media constantly pressure us to keep up with "The Joneses," an imaginary family that seems to have it all.

Want to know how fortunate I was? For years, I had the privilege of living right next door to my real-life "Joneses." Yes, that was their actual last name! But my Joneses were nothing like the Joneses mentioned in the Temptations' song. This amazing couple met as teenagers, fell in love, and got married when they were young. As of this printing, they have been happily married for forty-three years. Neither of them cared much about designer labels. They valued hard work and managed their finances wisely. Although they could afford it, they weren't keen on buying brand-new cars. They both had remarkable craftsmanship skills and remodeled most of their houses themselves. I'm not talking about minor repairs. I'm referring to major, high-quality renovations. They created a beautiful home, both aesthetically and spiritually, for their family.

The wife and I share the same ethnic heritage; she is Blasian, Black and Asian. More specifically, she is Black and Chinese. I call her my homegirl. My Joneses raised three wonderful, intelligent, well-behaved children who matured into responsible and successful adults. These Joneses weren't just kind. They were also incredibly generous. The wife cooked as though she was feeding a family of ten every day, and regularly shared meals with our family and others. Both her and her husband's cooking was exceptional! They would even try out new recipes on our family. We all happily served as their samplers.

On many Sundays, she would see me returning home and tell me not to worry about cooking because they had made plenty. I can still recall those delicious Sunday meals with a smile on my face. They were truly special.

Both the husband and wife were hardworking individuals. He worked for a major corporation, and she served as the CFO (Chief Family Officer) of their home, while also being a successful entrepreneur. They were both enterprising and both created multiple streams of income for their family. They maintained close ties with their respective families, and it was not uncommon to see multiple cars parked on our street when their relatives visited. Some of their nieces and nephews called him "Uncle Daddy." This couple was affectionate with each other, just like teenagers. They genuinely liked, adored, and loved one another, and they placed a deep value on their relationships with others.

Mrs. Jones possessed extensive knowledge of old-school home remedies and freely shared them. I had never tasted a mango until she introduced me to the fruit in my mid-thirties. I loved the taste so much that I bought a bunch of them and devoured a whole mango, from the flesh to the seed, eating it like it was a peach. Within minutes, my lips swelled up. I went to her and showed her my lips. She couldn't hold back her laughter, which made me laugh too. She diagnosed me with "Mango Lips" and explained that it happens when the prickly hair of the seed touches your lips. She advised me to bake the seed until it was dry and brittle, open it, remove the meat inside, crush it, mix it with olive oil, and apply it to my lips. It sounded like one of my mom's many home remedies, but I gave it a try, and it worked. That was just one of our many stories. She had solutions for numerous problems, children's scrapes, and ailments. She was fun, funny, and warm. Mr. Jones complemented her perfectly as a loving husband, a firm but caring father. They both worked hard and cherished their family.

"My Joneses" were the best neighbors anyone could ask for, and we cherished their presence in our lives. In 2005, Mr. Jones received a promotion, and they informed us that they were relocating to Pittsburgh. Each member of our family felt a deep sadness. We were losing family. When they put their house up for sale, I knew it wouldn't be long before we followed suit.

Those were the Joneses I aspired to be like. Yes, I confess that I liked (and still like) designer labels, and I've spent a significant amount of money on new cars because I have a penchant for the latest models and new technology. However, "My Joneses" had much more than material possessions. They possessed qualities that money couldn't buy. They were committed to family, love, support, generosity of spirit, strong work ethics, true partnership, spiritual grounding, and contentment. They weren't trying to compete with anyone or keep up with others, but rather focused on being the best versions of themselves.

Whenever someone begins to compare themselves or attempts to measure their worth against others, I always bring up "My Joneses." I still miss their presence in our lives, and I follow them on social media to stay connected.

While I acknowledge that I possessed many of the intangible qualities they had, I still occasionally battled the feeling that I wasn't enough. Reflecting on the past, it's now evident how

I attempted to find happiness and fill the voids in my life by looking outside of myself. Not to keep up with others, but due to an ongoing and unnecessary competition with myself. Their departure created a void in my life. However, their parting gift to me was the realization that my definition of success and contentment was not sustainable in the long run. This realization propelled me toward making significant and transformative changes in my life, despite the accompanying fear and discomfort.

Want to know the primary reason I couldn't keep up with the Joneses that The Temptations sang about? The pressure of juggling all those responsibilities introduced a level of stress that I no longer desired or needed in my life. This realization was quite an epiphany. Ironically, I made this discovery just after being promoted to vice president, which meant a greater time commitment and more significant responsibilities at work.

I'd spent many years trying to fit in until I realized that I didn't need to. Over time, I discovered that my family was "The Joneses." Not in terms of material possessions, but in terms of having what truly matters to us and being content with ourselves. We are the ones defining for ourselves, what peace, joy, struggle, and sacrifice mean in real-time. Sometimes it appears great from the outside, but just as often, it's messy. But that's the reality of life.

When I was younger, I was always looking ahead to the next step. Even when we lived in the "projects," I knew it was temporary because deep in my heart and my mind, I understood that my initial circumstances didn't have to dictate my outcome in life. This knowledge led me to make better decisions (most of the time), embrace sacrifice, and allow room for mistakes along the way. Could I have achieved more success? Undoubtedly yes, in terms of my profession and material acquisitions. Could I have been less successful? Yes, the likelihood of my being less successful was much greater.

Returning to the idea of comparing ourselves to others, I always say that I'm fortunate to know many people who have more than I do, and I also know many who have less. Yet, I cannot tell you that one group is happier than the other. From my experience, it's nearly impossible to sit and fully celebrate one milestone because human nature and society urge us to quickly move on to the next step.

The biggest problem with adhering to this societal script or succumbing to external pressures is that sometimes the decisions we make are simply not good ones. Sometimes the paths we believe are logical turn out to be illogical. However, we disregard those signs because we're fixated on reaching that next step.

Falling in love and aspiring to marry someone who has shown little potential to be the person we truly need in our lives, or with someone who cannot commit to a monogamous relationship, or who heavily relies on us without reciprocating that reliance—these are the decisions we make under the influence of societal expectations.

How many of us know people who got married simply for the sake of it, only for the marriage to end shortly thereafter? I can count at least half a dozen such cases. Similarly, I can count another half dozen instances where friends were in relationships but never got married. Others might view them and think, "Poor thing, they've never been married," or "It's sad that they never got married."

Yet, I look at some of these individuals and say that there's a good chance they dodged a bullet. Society doesn't grant us the leeway or grace to celebrate our avoidance of potential mistakes.

Today, I am delighted to see that our young folks are less focused on following "society's conventions," and are questioning the extent to which they want to follow them. They are more often doing things their way, however they are defining what that represents.

For me, that intense need for accomplishment and perfection has been a recurring theme throughout my life. Many of my female friends who were raised by Asian mothers can relate to this sentiment. It's that feeling of never being satisfied, no matter how much we achieve. It is tough to overcome and perhaps even impossible to shake. I'm not implying that this need for perfection is exclusive to Asians, but I can only speak from my own experience. Striving for perfection is utterly unattainable. Why? Because we can only control our efforts, not necessarily the outcomes.

We are mothers raising children—an undoubtedly challenging role. We manage marriages, navigate parenthood, and for some, deal with separation and divorce. We handle jobs, uncooperative people, careers outside the home, caring for parents, and for me, the added complexity of being a Black Japanese woman in America.

But here's why it's crucial to focus on ourselves and our progress. Worrying about others' opinions of us is a complete waste of time and energy. The truth is most people are so absorbed in their own lives that they only spare a moment to think about us before returning to their concerns. Not only is that a factor of human nature, its also why we shouldn't spend our time ruminating about others.

Looking back on my life, I now realize how much I fixated on that next step. I recall someone very close to me posing the question to me several times: "Are you ever satisfied? Can't you simply sit still and appreciate what you have?" At the time, I didn't fully understand the question, and it took many years for it to truly make sense to me. Human nature, and if we allow it, society, prevents us from sitting back and truly appreciating what we have.

The difference between most phases of my life and where I am now is my acceptance that I am enough and that I have enough. I focus on gratitude daily. I still face numerous challenges. However, by taking the time to practice mindfulness and active gratitude, my perspective has changed significantly. It doesn't cost anything except a little extra time to focus my mind and spirit on what I have. I don't count my blessings based on material possessions or accolades. I count as blessings my ability to manage my anxiety, and that I can celebrate the successes of our family, our children's milestones, and the good health of our elderly remaining parents, among other things.

The Joys and Challenges of Moving On Up

Throughout my career, I've had the privilege of working for some amazing companies that I truly loved. At Verizon, I had the pleasure of working alongside Linda Waddell, the brilliant woman who was a member of Mensa. Our connection was so strong that we still follow each other on Facebook to this day. I developed many other relationships at that company that remain strong today. At PECO, I formed invaluable friendships and found mentors who guided me as well. I am grateful for the strong foundation I was able to build with the experience gained from those companies.

In January of 2001, I joined Comcast Cable. My experience at this company was phenomenal in so many ways. I underwent tremendous personal and professional growth, embraced new opportunities, and had the honor of meeting extraordinary individuals who have made a lasting impact on my life.

Comcast provided me with a different sense of belonging. As likely the only Black Japanese Director at Comcast headquarters when I joined the company, I recognized the significance of my presence. As the company expanded, so too did my responsibilities, offering me the opportunity to travel and meet people from all walks of life. Managing partnerships across the US as well as in other countries further enriched my experience. Yet, what truly stands out are the friendships that developed and blossomed during my time with the company. Many of my colleagues became more than friends—they became family. Together, we faced numerous challenges and celebrated significant milestones in our lives, such as marriages, divorces, the joy of children, the pride of their graduations, and everything in between. We were pioneers in our fields, often stepping into uncharted territories without a manual to guide us. However, we knew we had a support system that always had our backs—a tribe that shared our experiences and understood our journeys. I believed that I no longer had concerns about fitting in.

Likely because there weren't very many of us, we developed strong bonds with one another. Most of those bonds still exist today. We are now spread out across the country and no, we may not get together often. But when we do, we pick up right where we last left off. Having our work tribe gave us a safe space where we could let our hair down. All of us were really adept at code-switching, but you can best believe when we got together, the masks we wore would be shed. It's hard to understand and fully appreciate the value of having that type of connection with those with whom you work. Many of us were first-generation college graduates and many of us were among the most successful in our respective families.

Some of us would hear the "you treat your friends better than you treat your family" complaint from our family members. The reality was that we had more in common with some of our friends than we did with some members of our families. They included similar values, lifestyles, and challenges. So no, I did not disagree with family members who said that.

Though our blood family members may have seen us sowing into our friends differently, they did not always have the benefit of seeing how our friends sowed into us as well. Many of us try to combat the "negative accusation" that we have changed.

Every time I speak with a group of young people, students, interns, etc., I tell them that they should be prepared to hear that. Especially as first-generation college graduates, or when they are "firsts" in any significant aspect of their lives.

The camaraderie we developed is a testament to the inclusive and supportive culture that Comcast also fostered. I will forever cherish the memories and relationships formed during my time with all the companies for whom I worked.

During my first year at Comcast, I was in New York when the historic bombings of the World Trade Center occurred on September 11, 2001. I was less than nine months into a new job in a new industry, so I didn't know very many people. I arrived on September 10th for my first National Association for Multi-Ethnicity in Communications (NAMIC) Annual Conference. When I got to the opening reception, I was a little disappointed when I realized that there was only one person I recognized. Sharon worked at Comcast in Government Relations. When she saw me, she ran up and hugged me, then took me around and introduced me to all the people she knew. She was wonderful. That night, I said a prayer of gratitude for my colleague, my job, my company, and for the impressive industry diversity of which I'd gotten a small peek that evening.

I awakened bright and early on the morning of September 11th to attend the opening session. As I could only attend the first day of the conference, I planned to leave late afternoon, stop by the box office to get the family tickets for a Broadway play for my youngest son's next birthday, and take the train home that evening.

The opening session began a little after 8:30 am to a packed audience in the hotel's auditorium. As the leader began delivering the welcome address, a bunch of our phones started ringing. We were asked to silence or turn off our phones. We dutifully obeyed.

I sat through maybe a half hour of the session and decided to go back to my room, grab my things and return to the session. Once in the lobby I turned my phone back on and saw that I had voice messages. I tried to check my voicemail but was not able to get through. I then went up to my hotel room and noticed the hotel phone's message indicator light was on. I tried to access the messages but could not.

I then called down to the front desk and couldn't get through. Why would I have messages on the hotel landline phone anyway? I reasoned to myself that the messages were probably not for me, since my family always called me on one of my two cell phones. Still, the message indicator light was not on when I'd left my room that morning.

You would think that by now that I would have sensed that something was off. But I just figured it was a busy hotel, and with so many of us there, the lines were jammed. I had also left the TV on but with the volume down. I looked up at the screen and saw a plane crashing into a building, but even then, just assumed that this was probably the news showing a clip from the past. It wasn't until I turned up the volume that it all started making sense. All the phones suddenly starting to ring during the opening session. No phone service in the lobby. No phone service in my hotel room. No access to the hotel phone's voicemail.

Now standing completely in shock and horror at this realization, I watched the replay of the plane crashing into what I learned was the North Tower of the World Trade Center. I rushed to call my family and my office in Philly to let them know what happened and that I was alright. Not surprisingly, I couldn't make a call out. I kept trying.

A little after 9 am I saw the second plane crash into the South Tower. Fear and disbelief gripped me, and I felt like I was frozen, watching the replay and ensuing aftermath. I recall thinking the first crash was likely an accident. But after seeing the plane hit the second Tower, it became clear this was not an accident. I was in an upper floor of a skyscraper hotel.

Was all of New York under attack?
"I've gotta get out of here."

I gathered my things as quickly as I could and waited for what seemed like forever for the elevator. Just as I was getting on the elevator, my phone rang. I said "Hello," and I could hear my then husband's voice just before the phone went dead. At least my family knew I was okay. After that, there was a flurry of activity.

Coincidentally, the hotel in which I was staying was in the Broadway section. One of its other locations with the same name was just across from the Twin Towers. This raised more alarm across our industry as it was the conference's official hotel. Fortunately, we were out of immediate harm's way. I had no idea what to expect.

I went back into the lobby and judging by the looks on everyone's faces, it was clear that everyone knew what had happened. All I can say is that we were all shell-shocked. I kept calling home and my office in Philly, and eventually reached my co-workers and let them know I was okay.

I learned that the conference leaders immediately ended the opening session and canceled the rest of the conference. Many of us gathered to discuss and process what was going on. Since the trains, planes, and virtually all forms of travel were shut down, we were stuck indefinitely in New York. We started walking around to Red Cross locations, trying to donate blood. We were trying to figure out any way we could help. I got to know many of the members of NAMIC as we all bonded together with a shared commitment to support in any way we could. These people who had been mere strangers to me less than twenty-four hours before, became friends, united around a common cause.

A group of us were headed toward a Red Cross location when we got a message asking us not to come, as all locations were overwhelmed with volunteers. That was a great problem. We walked the streets together. I'll never forget the looks on some of the people's faces who were covered in soot and ash, but alive. We found an open restaurant and we all gathered there, awaiting updates.

A very short window opened where I was able to get on a train that day and head back to Philly. I was one of the lucky ones, as many of my colleagues would not be able to leave New York until days, and for some, over a week later. It's still hard for me to put into words how I felt that day.

One of the worst parts of it all was how my family and I later struggled to figure out how to explain what happened, to our children. I recently had separate conversations with my youngest son and my stepson, who were four and three years old at the time. Fortunately, neither one remembers anything about it.

As someone who has had to deal with processing trauma at a very young age, my family and I realized we needed to discuss this with them in a way that it wouldn't be remembered as one of the most traumatic experiences of their young lives. Parenting, especially under those circumstances, was hard.

This attack on the US shattered an assumed innocence we hadn't even realized we had. I'd certainly experienced my share of racism but was deeply disheartened to see this depth of hatred leveled at countless innocent human lives. Our lives were forever changed. But, life went on, and over time, we returned to some semblance of normalcy. The following year, life got even busier. I took on the role of developing and implementing a new national program across my company's entire operation.

I found myself grappling with a heightened sense of fear. I had a lingering fear of flying, but the fear came from my questioning whether I could manage a national program of this magnitude.

Why was I still plagued with such intense doubt in my abilities? I had been entrusted with the task of developing the program, creating a deployment plan, formulating and rolling out a training strategy, and devising a marketing and sales approach. As a decentralized company, I had to engage with and convince executives at divisional, regional, and local levels to embrace this program.

Despite accumulating a wealth of experience and achieving significant milestones drawing from my corporate executive background, multiple degrees, training, and strong track record, I was still afraid.

I could talk about all the things I did to overcome my self-doubt, but the truth was I took it one day, one week, one month at a time, and battled through my fear. In the year 2003, on the road for about eighty percent of that year, I succeeded in rolling out the program throughout the country. In 2004, I was rewarded with a promotion to vice president. Yes, I was now the first Asian African American female vice president at Headquarters.

That same year my mother-in-law died, which shook me to my core. Her passing left a deep hole in my heart, and even now, I still miss her presence.

In 2005, we moved into a new house, much deeper into the suburbs. It was a new world for my children, further removed from our support system and families who looked like us. By that time, I was not as concerned with fitting in, but it was just the beginning for my two sons. By that point, I had moved twelve times in my life, not counting college or graduate school. This was the second home for my children and their very first move.

This move was a huge change for us all. I learned right away that others' perceptions of what we had quickly influenced the playing field. When people perceived us as having as much or even more than them, they seemed to value us differently. Simply stated, when we appeared to be on the same financial footing as our neighbors who didn't look like us, they seemed to more easily overlook our race and ethnicity.

I recall an incident when my son was in the fourth or fifth grade. There was a little white girl he called his girlfriend. Among our friends in the neighborhood, I had a wonderful Jewish friend we'll call Cameron. Cameron was friends with this little girl's mother. She casually asked me if I knew my son was dating this little girl, and proceeded to tell me that she knew the little girl's family well. Her father was a prominent businessperson, and her mom was a stay-at-home mom.

Cameron shared that the little girl's mom was initially concerned about her daughter dating my son. Cameron didn't explicitly mention race but being one of the few black families in the area, I had a feeling that was the basis for her concern. After all, my son was a very good student and a talented football player. I think he was the team's quarterback. He came from a two-parent household - both successful professionals. And most importantly, he was a nice, respectful kid.

Cameron told me she allayed the woman's concerns by telling her we were a good family. She said she mentioned our successful careers, our nice home in the neighborhood, and that we were nice people.

After hearing all this, Cameron told me that her friend was

then fine with her daughter dating my son. Hmmm… I was surprised at how comfortably Cameron shared this story.

My immediate question to her was: "Cameron, what if I'm not okay with it?" Although I didn't bring up race explicitly, it hung in the air, and she realized how her story might sound to me. So, the only thing that matters is her approval? I am certainly not racist, but this did not sit well for obvious reasons, and I wanted to convey that point.

Despite his being Black, we share all these other things in common, so upon learning this, she's suddenly okay? The assumption that she could overlook any issues she had with race because we had common financial and economic factors felt unsettling. Money, in this case, became the great equalizer. Cameron immediately apologized and admitted she hadn't considered my perspective. There were other stories along this line. Most, unfortunately, were not as obvious as this.

The following year, I had a profound epiphany that brought clarity to exactly how important it was for me to make a difference and to inspire meaningful change. Throughout my career, I was fortunate to participate in exceptional leadership development programs. Among them were the Comcast Leaders Forum, the NAMIC Executive Leadership Development Program for Leaders of Color, and the Betsy Magness Executive Leadership Development Program for Women. These opportunities immensely enriched my life.

Each time I was presented with a chance to participate in self-improvement, leadership development or enhancement courses, I eagerly seized the opportunities. Each program left an indelible mark on me.

After completing the Executive Leadership Development Program for Leaders of Color in 2005, I participated in a follow-up session a year later, led by a facilitator whom I deeply respected. She instructed us to complete an exercise that proved transformative for me. She challenged us to write our obituaries.

Initially, I felt a sense of intrusion and even anger at the thought. Why should I have to contemplate my obituary? The instructions were to write as if my life had ended that very day. I looked around and saw my peers all engrossed in the assignment while I remained hesitant. My reluctance stemmed from my recognition of the imbalance in my life.

At the time, I had a wonderful suburban home, amazing children, a beloved cat, strong faith in my Buddhist practice, and a challenging yet fulfilling career. I was active in my sorority, had a great support system, and a cool social life. It became clear that so many of my activities revolved around me, my family and friends, but for all I'd done, I didn't feel I was paying it forward to others the way so many others had done for me. I realized I needed to give of myself in a much more significant way, by devoting more effort to helping others.

Consequently, I wrote my obituary twice. The first version captured the snapshot of my life at that moment, and the second represented my aspirations for the legacy I wanted to create. I developed a plan and right away began intentionally aligning my actions with my newfound purpose. I became more involved with my cherished alma mater Penn State, assumed leadership roles within my local NAMIC chapter, and accepted positions on nonprofit boards.

As expected, life grew more hectic. I would caution anyone against a sudden rush from fifteen to sixty miles per hour, as I experienced. To effectively manage the many priorities, I quickly learned to ration my time wisely. Looking back, I realize that I placed greater demands on others' time and did not always show sufficient appreciation for their support. I prioritized being there for my children, and attending their school and sports activities, even though I was not as involved in the behind-the-scenes stuff like practice and preparation. Because I grew up with very little and had to make sacrifices to re-pay school loans, fund weddings, cars and homes myself, I was determined to ensure my children would be in a better position.

I was probably too focused on long-term financial goals that would position them for a future where they could attend any college they wanted without the burden of debt. I wanted them to start their adult lives with a better head start than I had.

During this period, the concept of personal brand gained more traction. While I have always valued hard work and cared about my image and reputation, I initially rejected the term "brand" as it felt contrived. As I thought about it, I realized that many of my decisions and actions were instrumental in shaping my brand. My brand was being defined, with or without my deliberate action. I decided to be more intentional about it.

I was already doing a lot of the "right things" based on my values, work ethic, and true concern for others. Honestly, I still dislike that term, but I also know that the reality is your brand is being established and reinforced every day.

I loved mentoring others, both formally and informally. Sometimes, despite our best efforts and intentions, it was not as easy in practice. Between 2007 and 2010, a group of African American parents within our community came together to form a mentoring group to support and empower teenage boys and girls of color. The volunteers were largely made up of African American executives who lived in our area. Nearly all the children of the volunteers participated in this program, including my own. We however, encountered challenges when it came to recruiting some of the more disadvantaged children within our community.

The creation of this mentoring group was met with skepticism from the larger African American community, who viewed many of the executive volunteers as "short timers." There was a sense of doubt surrounding our long-term commitment to the cause. This skepticism stemmed from past experiences when well-intentioned individuals would move into our neighborhoods, offering assistance and opportunities, but ultimately fail to follow through or worse, truly understand the complexities of that community. We all resolved that we would be different and were fully committed to making this mentoring program successful.

The exposure the participants received was great. The school district partnered with us and referred students to our program. We took them on trips, helped them refine their speaking and writing skills, did a mock election at the same time President Barack Obama was running, and held many other enriching activities. A side benefit was that the volunteer parents also bonded with one another, and we created a small social group. It was a great time for us, and we felt confident that we were making an impact.

In the long run, we were unsuccessful at getting the young adults who would most greatly benefit, to participate consistently in the program. The community's initial skepticism proved to be one of the main challenges to our program's ability to reach its full potential. Looking back, I'm certain that the community leaders had good intentions. Their skepticism was rooted in their concern for the children. Compounding this concern was also this sense of pride, passed down through the generations in our community, that discourages some individuals from embracing developmental opportunities presented to them.

Sadly, after several years, our program ended up mirroring the outcome of previous volunteers' efforts. I applaud the adult volunteers who gave their best for several years. We now understood that it was not our predecessors' lack of commitment, but a combination of other systemic issues that presented obstacles to being able to make the full impact we'd hoped. Our children greatly benefited the most, but they all had access to other enrichment programs as well.

Disappointed but remaining committed, I re-focused my efforts around helping others within my industry, and within groups in which I was involved. I also resolved to redirect my energy and passion into the development of college interns at my company. I accepted invitations to join other non-profit boards, especially those whose efforts benefited young people.

I quickly saw how my efforts made a difference. I loved mentoring my team members, and especially young employees of color. Many of them experienced the same challenges I had when I was younger. Wherever I could help them to avoid some of the missteps and mistakes I made, I willingly jumped in.

My efforts started becoming recognized. This was not why I did it, but I embraced the recognition to encourage others in my position to do the same. There were so many unintended great results of my effort.

My sons were watching in obvious and not-so-obvious ways. They were the ones who opened my eyes to "code-switching" I was doing before I was even aware that was a thing. Around 2009, I was the sole recipient of a significant industry award and delivered an acceptance speech in front of my family, closest friends, and numerous colleagues throughout the industry. After hearing my speech, one of my sons approached me with genuine curiosity and asked, "Mom, how did you learn to speak like that?" I was taken aback initially, finding the question both amusing and confusing. The speech I had given was likely my most formal up to that point, devoid of any jargon or slang. I'd worked on it for weeks. I responded that it was simply how I spoke in a professional setting.

Not long after, I took my boys back to my childhood neighborhood, and we visited my best childhood friend and her family. As we interacted, old memories came flooding back, causing me to unconsciously revert to the dialect and jargon we used to communicate within our community. The boys were once again amazed at how effortlessly I switched between different styles of speech. The professional speech was more formal than they were accustomed to hearing. My interaction with my childhood best friend was a lot more relaxed, and showed how proficient I was at "Ebonics."

I guess my every-day form of speaking fell somewhere in between. I never gave it a thought until they brought it to my attention.

This experience opened my eyes to the phenomenon of code-switching—the conscious or unconscious act of alternating between different languages or dialects. This flexibility is a product of my diverse experiences and interactions throughout my life. Code-switching is not only a reflection of our linguistic competence, but also an expression of our cultural identity and the communities in which we belong.

Looking back, I am grateful for the moments that brought my code-switching abilities to light, which taught me to appreciate the richness and versatility of language, enabling me to embrace the power of effective communication in all its forms. We as people of color code-switch based on our environment so often that it comes naturally and often unconsciously. Layer in both my Asian and African American influences, and I was confident I could hold my own in any environment.

"You Can't Have It All, At Least Not All At Once."

My former employee and friend Henri must have said that to me about a hundred times. And I wholeheartedly believe it to be true. "Having it all" is a constantly shifting goalpost. No matter what "all" encompasses, it does and should change.

Except for my job, 2009 saw me struggling in every aspect of my life. Professionally, things were going well. I'd received another major industry award, got accepted into a prestigious women's executive leadership program, and my team was performing admirably.

Simultaneously, I was privately grappling with the challenges of balancing a demanding job, children, marriage, and travel. Moreover, I witnessed two people very dear to me go through profoundly traumatic experiences that forever changed them, and me. Despite all this, I maintained a composed and well-put-together appearance on the outside. Neat physical appearance, hair always done, always wearing a smile. I was "swanning" at full throttle. Yet, beneath the surface, those webbed feet were flailing wildly and at full speed. I was struggling.

I'm convinced that those who know you and know your heart, have a sixth sense, even if you are not sharing your struggles with them. Tina and Kandii saw right through me. They were there for me, constantly checking in, and always ready to lend an ear when I needed to talk.

During a casual breakfast with my close friend and work sister, Andrea, I again assumed I was successfully managing my "swanning." However, Andrea, seeing through my facade, bluntly asked, "Barb, what's going on with you?"

As I write this now, it's difficult to relay because it brings back those emotions. Andrea knew I was not okay. She came over to me, hugged me, and assured me that we would get through it together. Andrea has been a great source of inspiration to me as she has overcome challenging periods in her own life and emerged on the other side happier, stronger, and more beautiful. Her journey, or what I called "her kintsugi," included finding a new loving partner who became a wonderful husband and great bonus dad to her girls. In the process, she attained a more consistent sense of peace within herself.

One morning, Andrea called me with an opportunity she thought would be perfect for me. The organization that hosted the annual Odyssey (which deserves a whole chapter to itself for its life-changing programs), had partnered with Royal Caribbean to create a marketing campaign promoting cruises to a more diverse audience. They wanted to showcase the amazing experiences women could have on their cruises and feature them in their magazine. My mixed heritage made me an ideal subject for this project!

I, a Black Japanese woman, was chosen, along with my Japanese mother, to be the featured subjects of this incredible opportunity. All expenses were covered for both my mom and me. We flew to and departed from Puerto Rico, and embarked on a cruise ship that took us to six or seven Caribbean Islands. Cameras followed us around, capturing our experiences as we indulged in all that the cruises had to offer. It was a fantastic chance to spend quality time with my mom, engaging in activities like spa services, rock climbing, dining, and immersing ourselves in the best the islands had to offer. The timing couldn't have been more perfect.

I included my sister in this once-in-a-lifetime experience, and Odyssey and Royal Caribbean graciously agreed, with the agreement that I would pick up the additional expenses. Since it was important to me that she join us, I was glad to do so. The two organizations did an excellent job of involving her in many of the activities. It truly was an incredible experience. While I had taken my mother on many trips in the past, either as a companion on work trips or vacations, this was the first time the three of us traveled together and spent nearly every moment with each other for a whole week. We were accompanied by a talented photographer and writer throughout the trip. Because of the photographer's presence, people would occasionally approach me and ask if I was someone famous. That was quite thrilling. I would laugh and respond, "No, just an ordinary person."

I never aspired to be famous, but in full transparency, that experience of being in the spotlight felt pretty cool. It almost felt like a precursor to reality TV before its rise to popularity. All in all, it was an amazing experience, and I will be forever grateful to Andrea, Cheryl, the Odyssey crew, and Royal Caribbean for providing us with the adventure of a lifetime.

Upon my return, my anxiety and the pressure I'd been feeling were waiting for me. However, I came back with a renewed determination to tackle things one day and one challenge at a time. That year also brought many positive things.

During this time, I also became a member of an

international women's friendship organization, The Links, Incorporated. While I knew a lot of members of the Links organization at that time, I knew very few of the women in the chapter in which I became a member. My first experience with this group of women was when I attended a game night hosted by their chapter. I was pleasantly surprised by the warmth and friendliness of its members.

I felt welcome and accepted, and they showed genuine interest in me. Over the next few months, I spent a considerable amount of time with them and was delighted when I received an invitation to join the organization. Their focus on service impressed me, and the emphasis on friendship deeply appealed to me as well. The combination of those two factors influenced my decision to accept their invitation. Fifteen years later, I can say that becoming a member was one of the best decisions I've made in my life.

Late last year, while putting the finishing touches on my book, I stumbled upon one of my many unfinished journals from January 1st, 2011. My goal for that year was to create my destiny and make my efforts count in a big way!

However, destiny had a different plan in store for my family and me. The year 2011 was meant to be a significant year filled with major milestones. Starting on January 16th, I was set to celebrate my tenth anniversary with my employer, Comcast. On March 1st, I would mark thirty years as a member of Alpha Kappa Alpha Sorority. Then, in the middle of the month, I would celebrate my fiftieth birthday, and later that month, a milestone wedding anniversary. These were all significant achievements, and they were all packed into the first quarter of the year!

In my journal entry on January 2nd, in the fastest breaking

of a New Year's resolution ever, I changed my goal. I instead committed to take a breather, even amidst all the celebrations and milestones. Despite, or maybe because of, these milestones, I wanted to slow down and discover my "Ikigai." The Japanese term Ikigai loosely translates to "purpose in life." Many in the Japanese culture believe that focus on our ikigai is one of the keys to long life, good health, and happiness.

This is a silly thing, but I wrote in my journal that I yearned to experience the comfort of wearing cool, chic clothing and comfortable shoes every day. I even added it to my list of goals. I also wanted to relax and spend precious time with my oldest son Kendall, who was a high school junior at the time and would be heading off to college in a year. I resolved to pray, exercise, and take a moment to breathe. The closing line of my second entry for that year was, "The best is yet to come."

Little did I know that everything I had planned would be overshadowed by one of the greatest collective battles our family would face. In January of that year, my son got sick and had to be hospitalized—a condition that caught us all completely off guard. The illness was severe and required several lengthy hospital stays, as well as homeschooling. I was working full-time and had been traveling extensively before his illness. Naturally, everything came to a halt as our focus shifted to his recovery.

While my co-workers were aware that something was wrong, only a select few knew the details. As with any significant family matter, I chose to keep the specifics private, confiding in very few friends and relatives. This led to numerous theories, speculation, and rumors.

My incredible support system kicked in big time during this period. My colleagues at work were nothing short of amazing! They stepped up and filled in for me at meetings, created presentations, researched and prepared me for tasks only I could handle, ensured I never missed a deadline or commitment, and covered for me every step of the way. I have always believed that the best leaders surround themselves with people smarter than themselves, and during that challenging time, each one of them proved this to be true. I will forever hold them in high regard, and I am eternally grateful to every one of them. They know who they are.

We were also fortunate to receive support from many friends and family members. During this period, Kandii shopped for us, cooked for Kendall, and spent time with him at home, providing him with much-needed attention. Mom would sit with him, doing our Buddhist prayers and chanting with him. My friend (and his best friend's mom) Carol surprised him with a duffle bag full of games, magazines and books to keep him busy.

I recall one day I had an early morning presentation in the office and Bren's dad had a commitment that meant he would arrive at the hospital later. I rushed back to the hospital after my meeting, and in the course of our conversation that day, Bren mentioned a conversation he'd had with Aunt Tina. "When did you talk to her?" I asked. "This morning." Bren responded matter-of factly. To this day, I don't know how she knew we needed her to pop in that morning, but she did. That's friendship.

One evening a new vendor came to town to take my team and me to dinner at one of my favorite restaurants. My original plan was to visit the hospital after work to check on my son and then join everyone at the restaurant. However, once I got to the hospital, I decided to stay with my son and sent a message to them all expressing my apologies. I encouraged the vendor, who had never been to the restaurant before, to make sure he tried the "Dip

Sum Donuts." Anyone who's ever had them knows how delicious they are.

A few hours later, I glanced up and noticed someone at the door who looked familiar. When I looked closer, I realized it was the vendor, carrying several orders of the Dip Sum Donuts. He'd brought them to the hospital for my son and me. This gesture touched me deeply. Since their company had already secured the contract, there was no need for them to go the extra mile. They truly earned a special place in my heart that evening. I later learned that the rep who delivered the donuts had to cut his dinner short to make it to the hospital before visiting hours ended.

Though neither my son nor I were able to eat them, I think the donuts won us some extra points with the nursing staff, to whom I was sometimes pretty demanding.

There were too many kind gestures to recount. To this day, I am grateful to everyone who supported us during this challenging time. Anyone who's ever had a sick child (or loved one) can relate to the pain and desperation that you feel. This was the darkest period of our lives, though we worked hard to not show it. There were days when I'd see my son in pain and fight to hold back the tears. As soon as I'd get on the outside of his hospital room door, the tears would stream like a river. This swan struggled to keep a calm and confident façade. Under the water's surface was a much different story.

Then, winter turned to spring. After what felt like forever, my son recovered. This story was nothing short of a miracle, and I'm grateful that he continues to enjoy good health. I thank all those who showed support outwardly, as well as the many Buddhist members and friends of other faiths who prayed for his recovery.

Kendall was amazing and displayed immense strength throughout this ordeal. It was his junior year, when he was applying to colleges, writing essays, and preparing for and taking the SAT, among other key milestones. As both his dad and I spent a lot of our time at the hospital, there was so much he had to do without our help, and he was alone a lot. He handled his responsibilities and commitments admirably, and I'm certain this experience accelerated his maturity development and sense of compassion.

Before his illness, Brendan was a great athlete. He played many sports. After his illness, although he loved sports, he did not get re-engaged. Well, at least we didn't think so.

When Brendan entered high school, he tried a whole new sport with which neither his dad nor I were familiar, Lacrosse. He practiced at our home and taught himself to play. He went out for the junior varsity team in his junior year. He made the junior varsity team, and after a few games, was moved up to the varsity team. I had no clue he was even practicing until we had some problem with the gutters on the house. As it turned out, he had been practicing, and the gutters were clogged with lacrosse balls. Brendan went on to play lacrosse in his senior year. His inspiring story, as well as his effort, earned him a sportsmanship award at his high school graduation.

I'm happy to say that both sons are doing great, and have grown into strong, resilient, caring men. I could not have asked for more wonderful, amazing children.

That was a tough, life-changing experience. I was grateful Brendan recovered. I would then enter yet another sad and challenging life experience.

Ugh… Divorce.

I had everything planned out perfectly in my mind. I had meticulously mapped out every detail, even down to the artwork I would hang in the boys' rooms at what would become their other home. My oldest son was in college; my younger son had just gotten his license and started driving. Each had their own bedrooms, separate clothes at both homes, and gaming systems at each home. The plan seemed simple - they would go back and forth between the houses seamlessly. However, reality didn't unfold that way.

My goal was to take all the positive aspects, as well as the lessons learned from our past challenges, and build a life that gave more peace to all of us. In approaching this next phase, I again embraced the principle of Kintsugi, which involves accepting the beauty within the scars.

Acknowledging the brokenness of my life was the first step. For three months, I cried nearly every day. It wasn't a planned occurrence, nor did it happen at the same time each day. But even the act of crying was a great sign. It showed me how much I had grown emotionally. From a young age, I had trained myself not to cry, and for most of my young adult life, I refused to cry in most situations.

I recall when I was young, there were times when my two brothers and I got into trouble, if our mother couldn't identify the culprit, all three of us would get spankings. I would always go first to get it over with. Mom would give me the most hits, expecting me to cry. My stubbornness wouldn't allow me to, which frustrated her to no end. She would then move on to my oldest brother, who would start yelling out in pain, even before she landed the first hit. His spanking didn't last long. By the time she got to my youngest brother she would be worn out, so he would get away with only a couple of hits. I was too foolish to realize that I either had to cry or go last. I paid an extra hefty price for my pride.

Being perceived as strong and stoic has always been important to me. I say being perceived because I was so much more fragile on the inside than I let on. I always strived to maintain grace under pressure.

Have you ever seen a swan sweat as it gracefully navigates the waters? No, and I would not be the first swan to do so. Vulnerability used to be my enemy. I can't pinpoint exactly when I started realizing there was strength in allowing myself to be vulnerable. I just know that it was a gradual evolution, moving from the mindset of "never let them see you sweat," to permitting myself to be vulnerable and ultimately embracing my vulnerability as a strength.

The tears eventually stopped.

Initially, I didn't even notice. Then one evening, it dawned on me. I hadn't shed any tears that day. Come to think of it, I hadn't cried yesterday, nor for several days leading up to that moment.

The thing I learned about heartache is that it leaves when it's good and ready. My heartache wasn't yet gone completely, but the sharp pain was replaced by dull sadness and realization. In the stages of Kintsugi, this would be the phase following the shattering of the ceramic, where I started picking up the pieces and attempting to reassemble them. Metaphorically, I had recovered most of the fragments but had to find substitutes for the missing ones. This marked the point when I began settling into this new life, meeting new neighbors, exploring nearby supermarkets and restaurants, and indulging in both mental and retail therapy!

It was during this time that I read the inspiring book, My Beloved World by Supreme Court Justice Sonia Sotomayor. Her memoir completely changed my perspective on life. In her book, she coined the phrase "existential independence," which she started developing when she was diagnosed with diabetes as a young child. Like my parents, her parents were also young, had their own challenges, and were not emotionally equipped to deal with certain situations. In Justice Sotomayor's case, it was her illness. Her response was to research and learn how to manage this disease herself, even at such a young age.

"The truth is that since childhood, I had cultivated an existential independence. It came from perceiving the adults around me as unreliable, and without it, I felt I wouldn't have survived. I cared deeply for everyone in my family, but ultimately, I depended on myself."
- Sonia Sotomayor.

While this fierce independence served as a strength in so many respects, it was also a challenge for me in some of my relationships and made it difficult for me to ask for help, or to communicate when I was struggling. I realized that I made it harder on others to support me, and my exterior shell projecting this "mental toughness" made it hard for me to show exactly how vulnerable I was.

Slowly and purposefully, I reconstructed our new home,

striving to recreate the familiarity and comfort of the boys' childhood home. I prayed and did everything I could to ensure my sons were ok. The truth is, no one in a family experiencing divorce is completely okay for a while. Divorce changes everyone involved, forever.

I made every effort to minimize its impact on my children. I loved them and myself enough to endure what felt like the excruciating pain of self-inflicted wounds, without any anesthesia. Well, not entirely without solace. Alcohol became my chosen escape, consumed in significant quantities at different times. However, I felt so crappy every morning after I drank too much. Consequently, that didn't last too long!

Once again, I reminded myself that everything, good or not-so good, is temporary. Our relationship between misery and happiness is interesting. We all know people (even some who are close to us) who are only happy when they see us miserable and conversely, are miserable when they see us happy. I know that to be true about some people. It was true about some who were very close to me. This realization was quite sad. But the reality is - their reactions were more about their relationship and peace with themselves, than about me. That knowledge gave me solace when some friends' reactions to my confiding in them proved to be quite different than I expected.

It was also at this point in my life when physical, emotional, and psychological changes were taking place as I was hitting middle age.

As my new circumstances evolved, so too did my relationships. Brendan started spending more time with me. With Kendall away at college, our dynamics shifted, but in a positive way. While I couldn't claim to be happy every single day, I had reached a point where I was content. I had learned that "happily ever after" didn't necessarily mean being happy every day. It was about finding a balance and embracing the peaks and valleys within my life.

One of the most empowering experiences was redefining my reality. I could shape and reshape my experiences, perceptions, and expectations. I no longer felt the pressure to conform or fit into society's mold. Instead, I embraced my individuality and allowed people to align with me, or not, based on their values and choices. This newfound freedom liberated me from the constraints of societal expectations and empowered me to live life on my terms.

Along my journey of self-discovery, I more deeply embraced the importance of authenticity and self-acceptance. I now felt no need to seek validation from others, nor to conform to anyone else's expectations. Instead, I focused on nurturing relationships that brought me joy and fulfillment, while respectfully and quietly letting go of those that didn't resonate with the "new me."

This newfound sense of agency didn't come without challenges. I continued to face moments of uncertainty and doubt, as I questioned whether I was making the right choices. However, these moments of self-reflection and introspection ultimately strengthened my resolve to live my life on my terms.

Following my divorce, I made a personal decision that I would never re-marry. At that point in my life, I found solace and fulfillment in focusing on the well-being of my children who were on the cusp of adulthood, nurturing my career, and embarking on a journey of healing, self-discovery, and peace. While I would eventually be open to dating, I decided that remarriage was not in the cards for me.

This decision didn't come from a fear of commitment or a negative view of relationships. It was more about my personal growth and the lessons I learned from past experiences.

I also decided it was time to get some therapy and do the work to confront and work through my baggage. This decision proved to be crucial to my personal growth and healing. I honestly wished I had done therapy sooner.

It was also during this time that I decided to focus on sowing into and reconnecting with my friends and support system and put off dating again for a while.

I am a person who strongly values relationships. I always marvel at how I seem to have the best: best husband, best friends, best co-workers, etc. The key, I've learned, is not in trying to find the best fill-in-the-blank. My goal is to strive to be that best fill-in-the-blank. I didn't always have the emotional intelligence to feel the way I now do. I unintentionally sacrificed some friendships along the way. Some because I tried too hard; others because I didn't try hard enough. It was all a part of trying to find myself and fit in. As I have evolved, I have also learned to place my confidence in my instincts to let me know when it's time to re-evaluate or walk away from relationships that no longer serve me well.

It was an 'interesting" period in my life, as I tried to navigate this new chapter. Additionally, I was focused on ensuring that my two college-aged boys were coping as well as possible, given the undoubtedly stressful circumstances.

My greatest fear in life has always been returning to poverty, undoubtedly a response to the trauma of my earlier years. Although I never aspired to be rich, I worry about not having sufficient funds to sustain myself for the rest of my life. Where am I going with this?

The third significant instance when the universe provided me with an answer was when I contemplated leaving the company I held dear. While I wasn't passionate about my job, I cherished the company and relationships with my team members and colleagues. I was only nine months away from qualifying for early retirement when the company was undergoing a merger, which would have presented new and expanded opportunities for me.

I was thrilled and excited about embracing this fresh new opportunity. However, when our company walked away from the merger, I faced the prospect of returning to my former role.

"Man's mind, once stretched never regains its original dimensions."
-Oliver Wendell Holmes

The role now felt limited and unsatisfying, I knew it was now or never if I wanted to pursue entrepreneurship.

I recall nearly twenty-five years ago, my boss's boss said to me, "You have to be the one to decide when to step away from the table." It always stayed with me. I prayed about it over the next few weeks, seeking signs from the universe to guide me. Though there were note-worthy occurrences, there were unfortunately, no major signs.

Despite major apprehension, I decided to take a deep breath and take the leap. Within a week, I set the wheels in motion to negotiate my departure from the beloved company for whom I worked.

To be fully transparent, there were various other factors in play during that time that further influenced my decision. Nevertheless, the timing aligned perfectly. And then that annoying dream came back.

That recurring dream of falling returned. Throughout my adult life, I'd had this dream of falling off a cliff, but I never took the time to analyze its patterns or frequency. I did some research on its meaning, which suggested that it could signify a feeling of helplessness or lack of control. As someone who prides herself on maintaining control, it made sense that these dreams would occur during moments when I felt like I was losing control.

I had that dream of falling off the cliff, but never recalled hitting the ground. I always woke up mid-fall, shaken. However, the night after meeting with my human resources colleague to discuss my departure, I had that falling dream again.

But for the first time, I landed. I can't recall what led to my falling off the cliff, but the descent felt long and seemed to happen in slow motion. Eventually, I landed in a waterpark. Surprisingly, it resembled a long slide in a waterpark in another country I'd visited several times. The dream was so vivid that even nine years later, I can still see it. I interpreted it as a sign from the universe that everything would be okay, no matter what. And it was. And it still is. Interestingly, I haven't had that dream since I landed. It's certainly not because I haven't felt out of control in the past eight years, because I've had my moments.

"Embrace uncertainty. Some of the most beautiful chapters in our lives won't
have a title until much later."
- Bob Goff

Leaving the safety net of corporate America was a huge decision for me. I have always had a strong need for security, routine, and stability. My life over the next five years barely resembled my life in October 2015, when I left my beloved company and corporate America for what I believed would be the last time.

At that time, during a lunch with my dear friend Mel, I shared my plans to leave the comfort of corporate America and the company I loved. She was very surprised and supportive. She wrote a blog about this major move of mine, although she didn't mention me by name. Still, I was excited to read it. It was only when I saw her blog in black and white that the reality of it all truly hit me. Once again, I was stepping out on faith, just like I had done numerous times before.

It was both frightening and exhilarating. It was the ideal moment for me to again manifest my "Ikigai," or life's purpose. This chapter would represent the closest I came to genuine satisfaction.

The next steps in my journey would take me to many wonderful places, expose me to new situations, and introduce me to great supportive people. Along with these experiences came both life-changing struggles, as well as moments of greatness. They also instilled in me a new appreciation for life as an entrepreneur. Do we truly desire to "have it all?" What does "having it all" entail?

The final quarter of 2015 marked the start of this new phase in my life and the beginning of my life as an entrepreneur. My sons had the privilege of calling two wonderful places home. I had managed to accumulate a more than adequate nest egg, had minimal debt, and could still travel and enjoy myself within reasonable limits. The boys were well-prepared for their college education with scholarships, dedicated funds, and their earnings from part-time jobs, ensuring they would graduate without any financial burden. They both had cars that were paid for, and trust funds their dad started for them when they were young.

At this point, I was beyond excited and ready to transition from a corporate executive to an entrepreneur. To mark this significant change, I embarked on a once-in-a-lifetime trip to Italy with some of my closest girlfriends. It proved to be an incredible experience, allowing me to transition from "Corporate Barb" to "Entrepreneur Barb." I explored business prospects, gained valuable insights, and created unforgettable memories with my friends. It was a truly remarkable journey. Upon returning home, my excitement and motivation to launch my company soared even higher. The moral, financial, and physical support I received during the early stages of my venture was truly remarkable. The company was off to a good start.

I loved what I was doing, was pretty good at it, and felt that the world needed it. Unfortunately, the financial aspect was much more challenging. Consequently, I took on more and more work to fulfill my need to make money, which resulted in the constant transformation of my business. I was busy but loving it all. That is, until I hit a major unexpected bump.

The bottom literally fell out of my well-thought-out plan. Again. In the spring of that following year, I experienced a period of homelessness. Yes, homelessness. All I will say is that it wasn't an issue of finances. It was a finite period, three months, but I had already moved out of my second home.

I immediately began scrambling to find a short-term lease. Fortunate for me, both Tina and Yaz invited me to stay in their homes. I also had surgery scheduled that spring, and at the same time, I was putting all my energy into setting up my new business. Emotionally, I was "recalibrating," so I thought it best to find a place to settle and decompress with as much quiet and solitude as possible. With all that I was going through, I wanted to spare Tina's family my drama. Yaz lived alone, worked downtown, and traveled frequently. Her home was the better option that caused the least amount of disruption to all involved.

My first week or so after moving into Yaz's, I was healing from surgery, and all zonked out on pain meds. My amazing girlfriends took turns visiting with me, sitting with me, and once I started healing, walking with me. This pause in my life was cathartic and peaceful. Everyone should give themselves a pause, no matter how brief, to reset their systems, just as computers do.

The universe stepped in once again. Yaz and I were both recovering from different things, in different ways. We spent hours talking about everything, and nothing. We experimented with food and did a lot of online shopping. I introduced her to blue claw crabs and forgot to tell her not to eat the part they call the "dead man," the spongy-looking gills on the underside of the crab. At least we learned they were not poisonous, because she ate them and fortunately, didn't die!

Although that experience that summer was one of the best

of my life, I was embarrassed about my living situation. Though temporary, I had gone from two homes to none, almost overnight. Though I don't think we ever discussed it, both Yaz and I shared my living situation on a "need-to-know" basis with others, so very few people knew where I lived that summer.

I can recall one incident when two of Yazzy's friends, - a former coworker, and a mutual friend came over to pick Yaz up to go out. I made sure I'd left the house before they got there, as I was embarrassed and unwilling to explain why I was there. I drove around for a while and came back after I thought they had left. They were still there when I returned, so I drove around some more. The best way to describe how I felt was awkward. Physically, and emotionally awkward. Embarrassed.

And it got even more weird. I was parked in front of a row home in Mt. Airy, listening to music and biding my time. A woman came out of the house and began staring at me. She stood there for about five minutes, just watching me. I finally turned down my music, rolled down the window and asked her if she minded my parking there. She asked me who I was. I can't recall what I said, but I remember thinking, "that's a weird question." She then went back inside, and I rolled my window back up and turned my music back up. She came back out, yelling at a man who followed her out. She began pointing at me. I again rolled the window down to hear what she was saying. She was yelling, asking him who I was. He said repeatedly that he'd never seen me in his life. I told her I was just parked there waiting for something and I'd never seen that man before. She was still yelling when I started my car back up and drove off. What the heck just happened!?

To the man who appeared to be in trouble, if you are reading this book, I'm sorry for picking the wrong parking spot!

Of course, my unquiet mind can always come up with possible explanations. I surmised that the woman thought I may have been her man's side chick? But parking in front of his house is pretty brazen, even for the bravest side-chick.

If I had told her the actual reason I was there, that would likely have made matters worse. I was a well-dressed temporarily homeless woman in a late model Porsche SUV, waiting for my friend's guests to leave her home so they wouldn't know I was staying there? I wish I could say this was fiction.

I then called Yaz to get an idea of when they would be leaving. She informed me that they changed their plans and decided to hang out at Yazzy's. I decided that going back to the house was the better alternative.

I entered the house and upon seeing the three of them, activated my best fake, extra-high-pitched overly enthusiastic tone and said hello to everyone.

My dear Yazzy sensed my embarrassment as I headed up to my room. She invited me to join them. The two others encouraged me to join them as well. I reluctantly agreed. Five minutes after I joined them, I was so glad I did.

All four of us ended up watching Beyoncé's new Lemonade video album together on a small smartphone screen since we couldn't get it to project on any of Yaz's huge TV monitors. We threw some food together and ate, drank, and shared stories. We empathized with Beyonce's pain, each shared what we were going through, and encouraged one another. What began as a very awkward experience ended up being such an awesome one. I wish I could have bottled up that mixture of non-judgmental, kind support we all gave one another on that day. To this day, I'm so glad I didn't hide in my room.

That incident shined a spotlight on the state of my psyche. I'd experienced so many peaks and valleys throughout my life. I had accomplished so much, and my track record spoke for itself, right? I'd thought I had long ago overcome my concern over what others thought, but I clearly had not.

Others' perceptions of me really did still matter. A lot. I had to remind myself that I was once again in the midst of a major transition. The caterpillar in her cocoon, on the verge of once again transforming into a butterfly. This realization provided me with renewed hope. I continued to push forward. That brief "homelessness" ended up being one of the best periods of my life.

And Then My Dream
Came True.

That summer, with the help of my incredibly supportive friends and my amazing network, I launched my company at the location of my former employer, Comcast.

My dear friends Tracy and Steve were owners of a Black-owned Eyewear Boutique and were tenants in the building. Tracy almost singlehandedly coordinated this event, which we combined as a celebration of their company, Omega Optical's sixteenth anniversary.

The support we received during the company launch was overwhelming. Friends, family, industry professionals, politicians, community leaders, fellow entrepreneurs, and other esteemed guests gathered to witness the beginning of my entrepreneurial journey. The atmosphere was filled with enthusiasm and a shared belief in the potential of this new venture.

It was a testament to the hard work, dedication, and countless hours invested in bringing my vision to life. The event was meticulously planned and executed by Tracy, who ensured that every detail reflected the essence and values of both my company and those of Omega Optical.

The Comcast Center, with its elegant setting and state-of-the-art facilities, provided an ideal backdrop for the launch. The venue's sophisticated ambiance lent an air of credibility and professionalism to the event, leaving a lasting impression on all who attended. This event marked the beginning of an exciting chapter filled with opportunities, challenges, and most importantly, growth.

Less than one year before this milestone moment, I had left my job at an amazing company, moved out of my sanctuary, and started a new business, and gotten divorced. In my mid-fifties, I was starting over, and with a hell of a lot less.

Those swan feet were paddling furiously beneath the calm waters. At the same time, I felt incredibly happy and hopeful. I was once again pulling all the pieces of my life together and creating yet another new piece of artwork, Kintsugi-style.

I approached dating cautiously, adopting a "dip my toe in the water" approach. After being out of the dating scene for several decades, I must confess that I was out of practice. I took great care in guarding my emotions, being mindful not to rush into anything prematurely. Initially, my mindset was geared toward finding reasons to rule out potential prospects, rather than seeking out their positive qualities. I liked the excitement of getting to know someone new. I also wanted to once again experience the flutter of butterflies in my stomach, always a good sign for me in the early stages of a potential relationship.

I found the few dates I went on enjoyable. Of course, I kissed a few "frogs," but I also dated a couple of genuinely good men. Sadly, I wasn't in the right mental or emotional state to truly appreciate their positive qualities. Looking back now, I can't help but feel sorry for those whom I dated shortly after my divorce. During that period, I carried unresolved baggage that I hadn't yet confronted, nor dealt with. I hated the break-up phase and was horrible at it.

I was also so busy that I didn't feel I had time for a relationship. I don't think I'd ever worked as hard as I did in that year. I worked on my business, on healing my family, and most importantly, on myself. I worked on rebuilding my life differently and redefining myself professionally and personally.

It was important to me to keep my personal life as private as possible. During this period, I encountered a few nice guys, but my heart and spirit were just not ready. There's one specific guy to whom I still owe a deep apology. Great guy, poor timing. The truth was - I needed to get myself together, make sure my boys were okay, and create yet another new normal.

I think about some of the things I said and did during that period and shake my head. There would be times when my unresolved baggage would surface in reaction to something innocent that occurred. I'd read way more into it and I'd take it out on the guy. Unfortunately, the poor guy had no clue what was going on inside my head. My moods would fluctuate, and I might have even picked a fight, or worse - gone silent. He'd invariably assume he'd said or done something and blame himself. The reality was it was just bad timing, and I wasn't ready. It was also at this point that I invested in some additional therapy to help me navigate the many changes I'd made that summer, to deal with the feeling of being overwhelmed, and to deal with the emotional baggage that I'd never fully addressed.

At the end of that year, I rewarded myself with a "work and play" trip to Paris, with my very own tour guide and translator, Yazzy. It ended up being a "life-purpose-redefining" trip for me.

While in Paris, Yaz, who was doing some self-development and working with a company that specialized in this work, shared with me a homework assignment she had been given. The charge was to create a list of the five most important things she was seeking in a mate. Sounds pretty simple right? And in fact, I think it is. I used to discourage everyone who asked me, to avoid creating "lists." Lists are so hard to live up to.

But her assignment was to list the five basic things that, at a minimum, your ideal mate must have. I would even assert that my five characteristics and behaviors should be table stakes for any relationship.

I came up with the following five characteristics:

1. *confident*
2. *family-oriented*
3. *spiritually- grounded*
4. *intellectually curious*
5. *open and willing to grow.*

For me, these were simple characteristics that I also believed I brought to relationships. I felt fully deserving of receiving them as well. Of course, the physical and emotional chemistry was a given. Once I completed my list, I vowed that I would not waste any more of my time, or others' time trying to force-fit anything. At that time, I decided to stop dating, fully confident that when a relationship was in the cards for me, the universe would give me indisputable signs, as it had always done.

I returned home from Paris with a new determination, merchandise for the business, and the resolve to paddle those swan feet even harder. Life felt good, and I was once again settling into another level of my new normal. All the right things felt like they were falling into place. It was not the big things, but a series of seemingly routine things that would soon take some unexpected turns, that would lead me to "that post" that everyone still remembers.

I mentioned my motivation for writing my book. During that year, amidst all the great things that happened, my life fell apart a few times. "That post" was written and shared a week after life had just straight-up kicked my butt. I debated with myself and went back and forth on whether to share, as social media had always been for me my "happy place." But I decided to do so to let my friends know how much they helped me (most unknowingly) get through one of the most challenging weeks of my life. It was also intended to be a message for those who didn't know me well, whom I may have unintentionally given the impression that my life was all (or mostly) rosy.

A week before Thanksgiving, a long and painful situation in my personal life came to an end. Reeling from the outcome, I drove myself home, got in bed, turned off my phones, and pulled the covers over my head for the next two days. It was something I had never done before. I had never felt that badly in my life. I felt that I was entitled to mourn. I was angry, hurt, disappointed.

What forced me out of bed? My commitments. At first, I lamented that I had so many previous commitments that kept me from staying in bed and continuing to feel sorry for myself. But it was those commitments that helped me get through the week. The bottom line was, I got up because I had no choice. In retrospect, I appreciated having every one of those reasons to get up. Because every day I felt a little better, though the sadness and anger lingered for a while after that week. My favorite holiday, Thanksgiving was the following week, and it was important to me that I begin preparing for it.

But more importantly, it signaled that it was time for me to turn the page and begin yet another new chapter of my life. I realized that I had only lost "stuff," and my CORE remained intact! I found a way to put it all in perspective, found a way to forgive, and agreed to let karma do its thing. I had full control of what happened from that point on.

As I mentioned, the response was so overwhelming and positive that after a few hours, I hid the post. I was uncomfortable with the level of support I received for actually daring to show my vulnerability. What the overwhelming response communicated to me? Don't be too strong to fall apart. What happened next completely caught me by surprise.

In the beginning of October, this man sent me a LinkedIn request. I looked at his profile and didn't recognize him as someone I knew, then viewed our mutual connections, and seeing many, accepted his invitation. Maybe he was looking for a stylist. A week or so later, he sent me a FaceBook request. Now that's getting a little personal, I thought. I accepted the friend request.

Our initial communication occurred when he, as the young folks say, *"slid into my DM."* One of the first messages I received was a private message he sent to me in response to "that post." It was a kind, well-written, sincere message. I responded by thanking him. We exchanged surface-level messages a few times after. Exactly two months to the day after that initial connection, we met for a casual lunch (he didn't call it a date) at a local restaurant.

On the day of our lunch, I arrived early. I ran into several people I knew at the restaurant. My dear friend SJD was meeting a friend, and when I saw her after having not seen her for months, I ran up to her excitedly. We hugged one another and began catching up. I'd arrived about fifteen minutes early. In my excitement upon seeing SJD, I completely forgot to go into the ladies' room, check my lipstick, and make sure every hair was just right.

So when he walked into the restaurant, I was not prepared. I was nervous like a teenager, even though it was just a casual lunch. He said he thought he sensed disappointment in my reaction.

It was simply sheer nerves. Once we sat down, I saw my friends Tina and Eric Coombs having lunch with their daughter. I went over and said hello to them.

By the time I sat down in my seat, I had regained my composure. This gentleman Michael and I had a nice long lunch, and I tease him to this day about his ordering three cups of coffee and three desserts to keep the afternoon going.

Michael shared that my name had first come up in a conversation with three young (he emphasized young) ladies at a Links event. He couldn't recall any of their names. I assumed it was Henri, a dear friend, and member of the Links chapter that hosted the event, who'd regularly "suggest" single male "prospects" to me. She said no, it wasn't her. In the weeks following our lunch, I would do some detective work and eventually figure out who the three women were.

Michael and I had what was probably a normal afternoon of getting to know one another. Very light chatter. At one point he mentioned how his female friends were always asking him to introduce them to his male friends who were like him. He then made a statement. "I'm probably the best man I know, and I wouldn't introduce myself to anyone." I thought that was kind of odd, but I sort of got what he was saying.

Heck, I thought I was a pretty good woman, but as I look back, I would not have introduced myself to anyone several years earlier, and before I did the necessary work on myself. He invited me to a mutual friend's holiday party that was being held that day. As I was ultra-private about who I dated, I thought it was a little soon for us to be going to a party together, but I still agreed to go. When we arrived at the party, though neither of us planned it out loud, he allowed me to go in first. And then he entered.

The mutual friend was Joe, who seemed happy to see me. I wasn't officially invited, but because we had known one another, and had many mutual friends in common, it didn't seem unusual that I would be at his party. Despite us keeping our distance, our friend Carl made the connection that Michael and I may have come together. He didn't say anything. He just gave us both that knowing look. Michael and I both greeted people separately from one another. After maybe an hour or so, I walked out and after a couple of minutes, he came out.

When we got down to the lobby, he pulled out one of his business cards and wrote his cell number on the back of it. He said, "I know what you've been through. Feel free to keep in touch. Call me if you ever want to talk." I responded with a polite "Okay." We shared a friendly hug and went our separate ways. I'd had a good afternoon with him, liked his energy, and decided even if it didn't go any further, he was someone with whom I would have liked to remain in contact. I'll admit that I was puzzled with the whole "business card and casually encouraging me to feel free to give him a call" move. I didn't know if that was new school dating. Maybe I misread the other cues. Though I said "okay," I also knew that I would not be the first to call.

I just grew up in a different era. I can be as feminist as the best of us, but believed if he was interested, he would reach out. If he didn't? Well, it was a nice lunch and an enjoyable afternoon.

He reached out later that evening. Our story genuinely unfolded like a fairy tale. Within no time, I was falling deeply in love. It's that feeling when you're convinced that every song you hear was written for you and your beloved? That was us. We would constantly (and still do) send songs we'd hear that reminded us of one another, and our love. It felt as though the universe was continually conspiring in our favor. Right from the start, we became inseparable. Despite living in different cities, we took advantage of every opportunity to be together. We each spent our first holiday season with our respective children, but we spent hours on the phone like teenagers.

One evening I came across a song that felt like it had been written exclusively for me by one of my favorite singers, Leela James. Every word resonated deeply within me. It posed a simple yet profound question: "Will you catch me if I fall for you?" I sent the song to him. I realized that if his feelings weren't as serious as mine, I needed to protect myself and gracefully step away before falling any deeper.

His response to my message was a single word, but it spoke volumes - YES. Dating him was, to put it simply, easy. His confidence, calm demeanor, concern for me and others, and ease with which he communicated amazed me.

However, his brilliance intimidated me. I had always found myself drawn to intelligent men, and upon discovering that he was a Harvard Law graduate, I couldn't help but feel more than a small twinge of nervousness. That persistent imposter syndrome still lingered within me. I worked hard to not allow it to affect me. For all I'd accomplished in life as a corporate executive, multiple degrees, extensive travel experiences, diverse interests, deep knowledge of sports, and history of professional success, I felt confident that I could talk about almost anything. So why was I intimidated?

Despite my fears, our connection flowed effortlessly. I went back to my "list" and discovered that Michael "checked" off all the boxes with flying colors. When I shared the list with him, he responded that he thought those five items were essential in any relationship. As our relationship continued to blossom, I was overwhelmed with happiness and contentment, convinced that I had discovered a state of bliss that would shield me from ever experiencing unhappiness again.

Yet, now and then, a nagging doubt would resurface. This

felt too good to be true. I questioned whether I wanted to venture into marriage again. Given the baggage accumulated from my childhood and my experiences up to that point, I genuinely wondered whether I could be the kind of partner I wanted to be.

I believe that love should be effortless to an extent. By "effortless," I don't mean free from challenges. But relationships don't have to be a constant battle.

We introduced one another to our children, families, and friends. We traveled and had so much fun together. Exactly one year after I made my "list" while in Paris, and ten months after our first date, Michael surprised me, and himself with a proposal of marriage.

Perhaps it was the combination of excitement and exhaustion from conquering the five-hundred eighty-eight steps of the old Karavolades stairs during our vacation with Tina and Miko in Santorini, Greece. Or maybe it was the lingering afterglow of the amazing meal we had just enjoyed at the waterfront restaurant. One thing we knew for sure was that alcohol wasn't a factor, as Michael has never been a drinker.

It could also have been the effect of being on one of the most romantic islands in the world, surrounded by our happily married best friends who consistently serve as an inspiring example of the kind of relationship we wanted. Whatever the reason, I'll never truly understand what inspired him to get down on one knee in a jewelry store we casually wandered into, offering a ring he hadn't yet paid for, with its price tag still attached.

But in the most natural, sincere, and romantic manner, he asked me to be his wife. There were no pictures or videos, as one can't capture such moments until the merchandise is purchased. However, there was no need for visual evidence, as every single detail of that moment is etched deeply in my memory. Although taken completely by surprise, I joyfully accepted his proposal. Fast forward seven years later, and our love story is our reality. It hasn't always been without challenges, but it has always been genuine.

Michael called his children and mother right away. He'd been divorced longer than me and had been involved with other women before dating me. He was more comfortable with sharing the news with his children. Michael was my first and only serious relationship since my divorce. He was the only man I'd introduced to my boys. I was a little uncomfortable sharing the news with them just yet, so I waited until we returned home to tell them. Both boys liked Michael and when I told them he'd proposed, they both responded, "We just want you to be happy." After getting their nod of approval, we shared the news with family and friends. Everyone was excited and happy for us.

During this same time, Dad's health had taken a turn for the worse. Once again, I was reminded that happiness and unhappiness can exist simultaneously. At the same time I was experiencing these incredible highs from being in love and feeling comfortable with the way things were falling into place, I was also navigating this painful chapter of my Dad's life.

Little did I know that the last time my Dad called me "Baby Girl" would truly be the last time. Well, that's not entirely accurate. As his health worsened, his memory and ability to recognize people began to deteriorate. It all began with undiagnosed and subsequent untreated glaucoma, which led to premature blindness. Unfortunately, Dad was ill-prepared to cope with his loss of vision, which eventually resulted in a condition known as Charles Bonnet syndrome. This affliction occurs when the brain remains highly active and begins to produce hallucinations as it tries to adapt to sudden and significant visual impairment. Over time, this condition progressed to dementia, ultimately leading to an early onset of

Alzheimer's. This entire process unfolded over approximately five or so hard, painful years. By the time Michael met him, Daddy was barely communicative. Michael would have adored my younger dad - a charismatic, intelligent, humorous, and engaging man.

On Thanksgiving of 2017, the boys and I arrived at Daddy's with our usual boatload of food. I'd already told Mom Sandy that Michael had proposed, and I said yes. I planned to tell Daddy during our visit that day. I wasn't sure he would comprehend, but that wouldn't stop me. I walked in, hugged Sandy, and approached Dad for a hug, with my usual loud and cheerful "Hi Daddy!" In response, just like he had done countless times before, he affectionately said: "Hey Baby Girl!" As I hadn't heard him say that in years, I responded with total shock. I actually think I screamed! I might have thought I imagined it, but it was in the company of the boys, Sandy, my sister, and her husband.

After dinner, I told Daddy that I was marrying Michael. I think I somehow convinced myself that he understood since he recognized my voice and greeted me in the way he had so many hundreds of times before. Daddy would have loved Michael.

That did in fact, turn out to be the last time he called me "Baby Girl." It's incredibly challenging to witness our once-invincible parents succumbing to sickness and old age. We must grab, hold on to, and savor these moments with those whom we love. I'm so grateful for the many wonderful memories I have with both my late dad and Mom Sandy. Both of my parents were blessed with long lives, but none of us knows how much time we have on this earth. If fortunate to live long enough, most of us will inevitably face similar situations. What I can say, is that it grounds you uniquely and profoundly.

Michael and I were married in August of 2018. I could write a book about all the things that transpired, starting with a sudden weather change from an expected beautiful sunny day to one that gifted us monsoon-like weather. The beautiful garden wedding in the gazebo quickly switched to an indoor wedding where we instead got married on the dance floor. Many of our friends traveled in severe weather, as it took place during Martha's Vineyard's peak vacation week. That was unintentional, and we were both sorry and deeply grateful that all but two close friends came.

My house sold more quickly than I expected, forcing us to have to scramble to find a temporary home and move two days after our wedding. My youngest son tore his ACL the day after the wedding, so my new hubby and I had to fit in a trip to Penn State's main campus three days after our wedding. I had to drive his car up, and Michael followed to drive me back home. There were many other unforeseen instances. Despite it all, our wedding day was, in a word, perfect. We had promised ourselves that no matter what happened, our wedding would be perfect. It was indeed perfect.

The icing on the cake was that once we finally got to our honeymoon destination, Michael planned the most beautiful and intimate beach wedding ceremony with our Besties Tina and Miko as Matron of Honor and Best Man, and two other friends who happened to be on the island, became our attendants. It was indeed a magical time, and Michael and I happily settled into married life.

Shichiten Hakki -
Fall Seven Times, Get Up Eight.

Then the next year came. It is often said that everyone has at least one chapter they keep hidden, one about which we don't speak. I had a year-long chapter like that, one I didn't want to share.

Usually, when we hear someone talk about their "Year of No," we think of our determination to say no to others. However, my Year of No was defined by repeatedly hearing the word said to me.

Although it's now several years later, I still jest about my "Year of No." I encountered one "no" after another. Some rejections were understandable, while others seemed like perfect opportunities.

In truth, some were opportunities I probably shouldn't have even been pursuing. The last one felt like an ideal fit. Yet, they all ended with "no."

Starting that year, I was blissfully happy in my new marriage and had taken on a leadership role within my Buddhist organization. Things seemed to be falling into a nice routine. However, I continued to struggle with balancing my business and marriage. I honestly was tired of the constant hustle and the "feast or famine" aspect of the twenty-four-hour, seven day a week hustle.

Since I was not willing to take on the same level of responsibility I had in corporate America, I started applying for less senior positions. First, there was a director job where I interviewed well, but they were looking to invest in someone for the long term and told me they didn't feel confident that with my experience, I would stay. That was my first "no."

I then reached out to a dear friend to ask him to help me make a connection with an organization with whom I was interested in partnering.

He asked if I would instead be interested in working for an organization for which he had just accepted the top job.

Are you kidding me? It was a dream job in an industry I loved. I jumped on it. After an initial interview and visit, I heard nothing. I thought the interview and visit had both gone well. I followed up for weeks after. No response. After a couple of months, I accepted the silence as a "no, by way of ghosting." I was disappointed.

Just when I felt I had made peace with the loss of my dream job opportunity, I received a call from this same dear friend asking if I was still interested in working for the organization in a different capacity. Without hesitation, I replied, "yes." My friend told me this was the perfect job for me, and he would call to schedule an interview the following week. However, that set into motion another few months of ghosting. This type of rejection through silence doesn't feel good and can strain relationships. After reaching out a handful of times, I stopped, realizing this friend just didn't want to say: "never mind" or "we found a better fit."

Ghosting, in this context, proved to be far worse psychologically than receiving another rejection. When you keep following up and waiting, you're denied the chance to find closure.

You are also denied the benefit of knowing why you weren't the right fit.

There is nothing worse than not hearing back. Our minds, hearts, and spirits are all affected by ghosting. When did it become so commonplace for people to disappear without a word? In this case, I ended up losing one of my closest friends because for one reason or another, they couldn't say no to me.

Eventually, I found closure within myself. Then a dear friend reached out to me about an exciting opportunity. Honestly, after having faced so many no's that year, (three), I said: "no, thank you." But after reflecting on it and learning that the position remained unfilled for several months, I decided to throw my name in the hat. Making this decision to push through my fear of yet another rejection felt empowering. The more I learned, the more I felt like this was not just any job; it was THE job. However, after five weeks, multiple interviews, presentations, and what I thought were strong green flags, I received another "no." This "no" was clearly due to politics, where I would later be told I was used as a pawn. Learning that fact was more disappointing than hearing another "no." By that point, I had become somewhat accustomed to hearing "no." But it still felt like crap.

Before leaving corporate America, and even in my years as an entrepreneur, I had grown accustomed to receiving very few "no's" in my life.

Reflecting on that year and the three major "no's," it was probably one of the hardest, yet most growth-generating period of my life. It opened my eyes to the struggles many people face throughout their lives. It deepened my compassion for others. I learned to gracefully accept "no" and realized that if I truly trusted in my faith, these rejections were ultimately for the best. 'Support from Michael and my faith are what got me through those tough times.

I accepted that the universe was protecting me and preparing me for the best opportunities in my life. In most cases, I was probably not the best candidate. In the meantime, I learned a great deal about humility.

I'm not sure if hearing the word "no" ever gets easier. Hearing it so often hurt and impacted my self-esteem and my relationship with myself. I became increasingly critical of myself, striving to be better and better, resolved to maintaining the best attitude while gracefully accepting defeat.

It was the end of the year, and that final "no" really stung. After receiving the call, I sat on my chaise in my office, took a deep breath, and let reality sink in. Then, I asked myself, "What's next?" I honestly didn't know. I murmured an R-rated version of "shucks" out loud and just sat, letting it sink in once again. The reason given? They weren't confident I would be as tough as I needed to be with the team. Hah! I'm sure all the folks who reported to me over the years would laugh at that.

Throughout my year of no, I was fortunately still able to earn money from my business, mostly through long-term relationships and loyal clients, referrals, and some dear friends. I was also grateful that the money I'd earned, invested, and managed throughout my long career in corporate America gave me a cushion as well. And when I beat up on myself, Michael would reassure me: "I got you!" I loved him for his support, but you know we independent women can sometimes have trouble with that.

"Makeru ga kachi" - English Translation: "Victory lies in defeat." This Japanese quote conveys the idea that winning every battle is not necessary, and sometimes losing is actually winning. I didn't feel that way.

But during this time, I learned that no matter our age, if we are committed to personal growth, hearing "no" is an inevitable part of that journey. Failures, in their purest sense, contribute to our growth. I prayed long hours to glean the lessons from them, but to let go of the psychological impact of hearing so many nos. I constantly reminded myself of the concept of shichiten hakki - "Fall down seven times, get up eight." And each time I fell, I willed myself to get up.

If you spent time with me during that period, you would have never known what I was experiencing. I was continuing to "swan," though disappointment shallowly hid under the surface.

Then I learned to say no _FOR_ me. While licking my own wounds from the rejections, I started realizing the value of my personally saying no to others for my own peace, benefit, and sanity. I'd heard the word "no" said to me enough times. I'd learned to accept hearing it. Now, it was up to me to learn to say the word to others when needed.

I am a natural problem solver and have always loved helping others. Over the years, my need to help others sometimes created issues for me. I often took on other people's problems, relieving them of the responsibility of resolving them for themselves. I'm not certain when exactly I began dealing with what I refer to as "fireballs." Do you remember playing the game "hot potato" as a child? It was a challenge to see how quickly you could pass the hot potato to someone else. Fireballs? It's the same concept. A fireball is a burning issue that requires assistance, and when passed to others, it becomes their issue. It becomes the recipient's responsibility to get rid of it.

Fireballs have been a part of my life for as long as I can

remember. Whenever my mom encountered a problem, or when someone (often a family member) presented an issue to her, she would immediately pass it on to me. She would drop it right in my lap with the full knowledge that she wouldn't have to worry about it anymore. It became my responsibility to put out the fire. When the fireballs were my mom's, I would take them on without hesitation.

Other times, they were fireballs she had accepted from other family members or friends. Due to my need to please, I would dutifully put out these fireballs, taking the worries off Mom's shoulders. I became so accustomed to doing this that it seemed normal. By taking them on, I enabled my mom to shift the responsibility of finding a solution from herself to me. These fireballs varied in size, ranging from significant problems like legal issues involving siblings or someone needing money, to smaller concerns.

On several occasions, I received calls from strangers who were friends of my mom's, seeking help with customer service issues related to the company for whom I worked. Mom didn't hesitate to give out my personal phone number, and I would receive random calls from people stating my mom had given them my number and asking for assistance with their customer service problems. Mind you, I didn't work in customer service. The third or fourth time she did this, I finally asked her to stop doing it.

As I grew older and took on more responsibilities such as marriage, children, and other things that required my focus, I began to question why I was always the one she expected to take on these issues.

My mom was loved by everyone. She had a natural talent for helping people, and I seemed to have inherited that trait. She genuinely cared about others, and I appreciated that. However, it was exhausting, and the more fireballs you take from people and resolve, the less inclined they are to figure things out for themselves. I realized that I had set the expectation by often helping to come up with solutions. When I started saying no to her, it wasn't well-received. Again, I didn't blame her for this.

Many years into my adulthood, I was still solving problems for Mom. It wasn't until I went through a particularly difficult time myself, that I started saying "no." Neither my mom nor my family members knew what was going on with me. I simply couldn't handle anyone else's stuff.

I sat Mom down and once again re-explained the concept of fireballs to her. I told her she needed to stop taking others' fireballs and passing them on to me. I also had to be disciplined enough to recognize and not accept them.

I asked her to consider a different approach when someone called her with a problem. I encouraged her to pause and ask herself, "Is this something that she (Mom) should be handling?" And secondly, "Is this something that she should be passing on to me?"

I sometimes advised her to give it back to the person who gave it to her. I'm sure I wasn't the only one of her children that Mom reached out to in this way, but I can only speak about my own experience. Up to the time of her death, Mom still occasionally shared her fireballs with me, but I didn't mind managing hers.

I very seldom shared my personal challenges with my mom, as she often just didn't have the ability to empathize with me. She could only see the impact on herself. I don't share this as a criticism, but rather as a reality to which I had grown accustomed. I recall one time when I was dealing with some pretty scary health issues, and I shared my concern with her. Her response was, "Get well because I need you." She never knew how deeply those words hurt. I knew without a doubt her response was not meant to hurt me. Yet it felt like her first concern was purely based on her own needs. I'm sure if I had pointed out to her how that landed, she may have realized. This "existential independence" that I'd relied on as a survival tactic as a child, young adult and now grown woman served me well in helping me to shield my heart. It also served to my disadvantage at other times.

Our relationships with our parents are so complicated. I recall an exchange while consoling a once dear friend to whom I'd occasionally confided about my relationship with my mom. She had just lost her mother, and I told her I understood.

She said, "You don't understand. My mother and I were incredibly close, so my pain cuts even deeper." The implications were that my mother and I were not close, and that her pain was somehow deeper than mine because her relationship with her mom appeared to be less complicated.

I can't think of very many things more agonizing than grieving the emotional disconnectedness with a living mother. Though this friend's words caused me pain, I reminded myself that we all perceive life through our lenses. Instead of taking offense, I realized that I couldn't walk in her shoes any more than she could walk in mine. The truth is, none of us can determine whose tragedy is more tragic. Mourning the loss of any parent is undeniably difficult.

I also got comfortable with saying no to other things that I didn't believe benefited me, my business, or my personal life. I stopped negotiating prices for my professional services. I began to say no to speaking opportunities where the "compensation" was exposure, and I began limiting the many hours of providing free coaching services. I still do pro bono way more often than I should and am sometimes surprised at how much of my time folks will take to get free advice from me, with no hesitation.

Thankfully, my year of no eventually came to a close. As we rang in a new year, I excitedly welcomed the opportunity to start fresh once again.

I took a planned break from my business for the first two months to finish writing this book. Though I made a lot of progress over those two months, I didn't make anywhere near the progress I needed. There were so many other things I found myself doing. Procrastination and writing can sometimes go together, and that's what I experienced. During the first two weeks of the year, I helped my son move to another city following a job promotion. I reorganized our home, engaged in excessive social media consumption, and did minimal writing. I almost convinced myself that maybe this book wasn't such a great idea, but I was already four years in! The end of February approached, and though I'd made a lot of progress, I had to return to running my company. I had work that was piling up, and I had clients with whom I needed to resume working or potentially lose.

At the end of my two-month break, Michael and I joined Tina and Miko for a weekend in the Bahamas. I figured this would be the perfect transition between putting the book aside and re-focusing my attention on my business. I was excited, but at the same time, disappointed in myself for my inability to complete the book.

It was also during this time that we began hearing about the coronavirus coming to the US. We started receiving warnings to avoid crowds. We had just proactively canceled what would surely have been a wonderful celebration Michael coordinated for a Girls' Night at the Sixers NBA game for my birthday.

On Thursday, March 12th, despite my worries about the highly contagious nature of the virus, I was determined to attend that evening's Sixers game. Sitting in my car in the stadium parking lot, I listened to the local sports channel debating about the responsibility of the Sixers management to cancel the game instead of leaving the decision to the fans. I spent a few minutes contemplating whether to enter the stadium that night. I eventually made my way inside. While walking to my seat, I passed a man who coughed in my direction without covering his mouth, prompting me to snap at him to be more considerate. He sheepishly apologized, and I regretted my sharp tone, offering a smile in return. It looked like most of the stadium was filled, but it was a far cry from most games' attendance, which are nearly always sell-outs. I still moved forward and just hoped that I would be safe. I stayed until the end of the game.

Thank goodness we did cancel the party though, as the day after that last game I attended, the NBA suspended the season until further notice.

If there was a silver lining, it was that Michael and I instead went to one of my favorite restaurants, Estìa, for my birthday. Unbeknownst to us, it would be our last dinner out for quite a while. We were the first ones to arrive at the restaurant and actually joked about this being the only time we could act like we had shut a restaurant down for a special dinner for the two of us. That didn't last too long, as another group came in.

As the hostess brought the family by us on their way to their table, one of the men turned my way and coughed without covering his mouth. This time I didn't say anything to him. But when the waitress came back, I asked her to replace our drinks and all the settings on the table. She ended up moving us to a new table. Little did we know that would be the beginning of some serious paranoia I would experience about COVID-19. We enjoyed a nice dinner, and I had a nice birthday.

Two days later, we were in quarantine. Professionally, I was in disbelief. After all, I had taken off two months to finish the book. I had just gotten back into the swing of things. Most of my business was face-to-face, so I didn't even know where to start to pivot my business. I decided to view this as a potential gift from the universe and committed to once again refocus my energies on my book with a renewed determination. It worked for the first few weeks. I would dedicate full days to just writing, and it felt great.

Then anxiety set in. My motivation started to dwindle. Some days I was successful in writing for a few hours. Some days I struggled to type a few words. I had so much to write about, yet I just couldn't bring myself to begin.

And then it hit me.

The fear of rejection had gripped me so tightly due to the countless no's I'd received over the past year. It didn't matter how much I had achieved in life, nor how much support I had from my wonderful family, loving husband, and amazing friends. I had accomplished so much and possessed what I believed to be an impactful story that could help others. However, deep down, the fear of writing this book and sharing my story terrified me to the point of inaction. Once I understood this, I challenged myself to write through the fear. In the first six or so months after quarantine began, I had found my rhythm of writing and supplementing my income by picking up virtual speaking and coaching gigs. I re-taught myself how to crochet. I bought an adult coloring book and began coloring beautiful pictures. I experimented with photography. I blinged-out sneakers. I did so much during that time.

But I had to remind myself of the purpose of this book. The swan looks like she's got it all under control, but the palmated foot-flapping below the surface tells a different story. I found all these wonderful ways to distract myself, but if my ultimate goal was to inspire others, I had to keep focus on getting my story written.

If I'm truly honest with myself, that's when my writing began to take shape. I realized that while this is a story about overcoming challenges and aspiring to create my best life, I was hesitant to share the pain I felt. Despite repeating countless times that happiness is a journey, not a destination, I was trying to put a positive spin on an aspect of my life that not only wasn't great at the time, but I felt like I was failing. I could hear the words of one of my dear friends in my head, saying, "Hey, you've already proven yourself. You've been happily married twice, successfully raised children, had an amazing career as a corporate executive, navigated through difficulties, and embarked on a second career. You don't owe anything to anyone." It was all true, but I owed it to myself.

As challenging as it was for me to resume writing, it was even more daunting to confront the possibility that my story might never see the light of day. That realization drove me back to the writing table, time and time again. I reassured myself with this thought: "You can write about all these emotions, and if you don't feel comfortable sharing them later, you can simply edit them out of the book. It's that simple!"

It was during this period that I had the opportunity to join my dear friend and mentor Grace Killelea's women's leadership development company as a consultant. She'd decided to pivot her successful company and transition to a fully virtual format. When she offered me the chance to work with her, I eagerly embraced it, and to my delight, found that I absolutely loved it. What surprised me was how comfortable clients were in engaging in dialogue and sharing their thoughts virtually. It opened up a whole new level of connection and interaction. Additionally, my executive coaching practice began to flourish during this time.

Coinciding with these positive changes, Michael and I were preparing to move into our new home we had been in the process of building before the pandemic struck. It was a significant milestone for us, and we knew it would bring a sense of stability and comfort during the quarantine period.

As time went on, I began to realize that this quarantine experience wasn't going to be as dreadful as I initially anticipated. The combination of engaging work opportunities and settling into our new home gave me a more positive outlook, and I started to see the silver linings amidst the challenges.

The universe presented me with another opportunity to reflect on how far I had truly come. In the summer of 2020, I found myself unexpectedly growing a garden, more than forty years after my first gardening experience. It all happened quite serendipitously when one of my Buddhist friends mentioned to me that she had a garden in our neighborhood. Intrigued, I asked if I could visit her garden and offered to help in exchange for some of her produce. That very same day, she invited me to join her. While there, I met the garden manager and shared my love for gardening and the experiences I had many decades ago when I had a garden as a teenager. He offered to give me a plot in exchange for my helping with the upkeep of the community garden. I couldn't say yes fast enough!

The following day I had two empty garden plots of my own. Caring for that garden became the highlight of my day, allowing me to momentarily forget about everything else happening around me as I devoted myself to growing my own fruits and vegetables.

If someone had told me a few years before that my future would involve managing a garden, harvesting organic vegetables, making delicious almond butter from scratch, experimenting with cooking, and finding joy in maintaining our home while pursuing the professional work I love, I would not have believed it. I loved being a half homemaker and half professional woman. The swan felt settled that summer.

Then in the fall, I lost my dear dad. That September, Daddy passed away. Though extremely sad, I was also relieved that he was no longer suffering. We planned a COVID-appropriate funeral. Besides close family members, most people had to attend the ceremony via Zoom. It felt great to see family members for the first time in a while. It was a time of sadness, happiness and finding peace within ourselves.

I grieved Daddy's passing and as I reflected on his life, I experienced so many feelings. The most prevalent feeling? Gratitude. In looking back on his life, I gained a deeper understanding and perspective on the true courage my dad had at such a young age. Both Mom and Dad were twenty-six years old when I, the third living child was born.

When my youngest son was twenty-six years old, he had been out of college for four years, was single, had a good job with a great company, and strong relationships with his family and friends. Like me, he has many friends from various walks of life and a strong support system. He is confident, a bit too emotional about sports in my opinion. But overall, he is a great and pretty responsible young man. At twenty-six, he didn't have anywhere near the level of responsibility that my dad had. I can't imagine my youngest son having a wife from another country who can't speak English, and three young children aged five, one, and a newborn. To be honest, I can't imagine my twenty-nine-year-old Kendall managing that much responsibility either. But that was a different day.

I have immense empathy for both my mom and dad. I didn't become a mother until I was in my thirties, and even then, I wasn't sure if I was ready. Are we ever truly ready?

Both of my parents have been the most significant influences in my life. Because of the challenges they faced, they spent long periods of their lives together, and sizable periods apart.

We then received news of a close family member's illness and their need for surgery. At the same time, we had begun the process of packing up to move into our dream home.

My business coaching activity had picked up, and I was also dealing with numerous requests for advice from friends and mentees who were struggling during the pandemic. Balancing work and the demands of setting up our new home became overwhelming.

Somehow, amidst the chaos, I still found the time and strength to comfort clients, and friends and offer encouragement. I was a little surprised at how comfortable that some friends were seeking coaching without offering compensation, considering that many of them had well-paying jobs and could easily afford to see a therapist.

But when my friends needed me, I prided myself on being there for them. Helping others actually helped me to get through challenging and uncertain times as well. I also joined what I referred to as social media groups focused on common interests, such as sports, gardening, cooking and home decorating.

My values and focus had significantly shifted. Here's what I didn't do during quarantine. I didn't finish writing my book. I didn't maintain my lifelong commitment to regular workouts, despite how much I needed the endorphins. I didn't launch my seafood salad business. I decided not to pursue a non-profit executive opportunity presented to me.

On the other hand, I accomplished a lot.

I successfully grew vegetables in my garden. I contributed to building a house and more fully supported my stepmother, who took great care of my dad until his death. I learned to make the most divine almond butter and roasted pumpkin seeds. I enjoyed fresh kale salad nearly every day. I decluttered my wardrobe, letting go of many clothes since I no longer aimed to fit into a size four. I discovered who my true friends were. I once again re-shaped my business, actively volunteered, and donated my time, money, and services.

But even in quarantine, the concept of fitting in resurfaced. I was nearly kicked out of a social media group because I was deemed "not black enough." It was during the pandemic when these social media interest groups started popping up. There was one group I joined because all the members liked shopping at their store, "Fisher Joe's." We discussed our favorite products, recipes, and stories about this chain. Discussions began to occur about keeping the group exclusive to "Black women."

They explicitly stated they didn't want non-Black or biracial women in the group, and that we were free to start our own groups. This made me question the concept of being one hundred percent Black, considering man's historical mixtures dating back to slavery and the intermingling of bloodlines. How do we determine our level of Blackness? Is it based on our physical features like lips or hair? And why should we be held responsible for something over which we had no control? I couldn't control being born to a Japanese mother and a Black father.

I dated and married Black men and gave birth to Black children. It was never about excluding others. I had witnessed the challenges my interracial parents faced in their marriage. I value diversity, as evident in my love and acceptance of our diverse family members and friends with varying ethnic backgrounds.

Before they could expel me from the group for Black girls, I expelled myself. In their logic, I didn't fit the criteria of being "Black enough." I've never believed in engaging in online battles, and honestly no longer wanted to be a part of a group with those views.

What was the most disappointing was that it happened on the heels of the whole Black Lives Matter Movement. I get that there are benefits to creating your own with like- and like-minded people. It happens all the time. But what was triggering for me is that it brought back a lot of memories and discomfort, once again begging the question: where do we Biracials fit in?

I grew up exposed to both Asian and Black cultures, though primarily the Black community. Our family lived in predominantly Black neighborhoods and had Black relatives. Our neighborhood "aunties and uncles" were mostly Black. I became a member of a Black sorority and other organizations composed mainly of Black individuals. However, I wasn't exclusive to just those groups. I was involved with other diverse groups as well. I just came across my membership certificate as a member of Alpha Phi Omega, a co-ed service fraternity at Penn State.

Anyone from any ethnicity can attest that there's a unique kind of connection we share with people who have a similar background. There's a delicate balance between having something exclusively for us and discriminating. The irony of it all is the fact that we as a culture have, and continue to, fight so hard for inclusion. Yet we proactively exclude others whom we don't think have enough Black in us. I truly hope someone who was part of that charge reads how this feels on the other side. I joined a less exclusive "Fisher Joe's" group of which to this day, I enjoy being a part.

At the same time, the Black Lives Matter (BLM) movement brought about changes in not just the US, but other countries as well. I was encouraged to discover that BLM positively impacted my Asian culture as well. One major Japanese Cosmetics company dropped the word "bihaku," meaning "beautiful white" from its marketing efforts. There were other such efforts where a group of Japanese brands banded together in protest of injustice.

Beauty Found in Impermanence and Imperfection

By this point, I had found a steady sense of contentment in my life. We'd successfully adjusted to quarantine and were now getting out a little more. I was engaged in the most fulfilling work of my life, thanks to GKC and YMWIC, and many faithful clients.

Sixty days before my sixtieth birthday, I set an intentional goal to create value every day by engaging in a different activity that would benefit either myself, my loved ones, or society. I invited my "people" to contribute their ideas. I called it my sixty-by-sixty commitment to myself.

The daily activities and journey were both amazing and demanding, requiring a lot of energy. Some of the daily activities were small, like dancing by myself to my favorite music for a full hour and dressing up as Shuri, the superhero from Black Panther. I wrote a "just because" love note to my husband and expressed my love to my dear friend Andrea through a heartfelt letter. I gifted a timely and relevant book to my friend Gab and, in return, received one from her a month later. I took long walks with my love, kicked off a sixty-day intermittent fasting program, and hiked four miles just to get cream cheese. Don't ask why! I pulled an all-nighter to create blinged-out sneakers for my bestie Tina, hung long-overdue family pictures, and completed the design of my office. I moderated a COVID vaccine Town Hall to educate the community, received and shared an amazing family collage from my cousin Tracy, and had an incredible photoshoot with my dear friend and magic-maker, Whitney The Great. I played hockey, spent a full day with my bonus mom Sandy, and crafted "My Intent bracelets" as meaningful gifts for my family and closest friends. I re-learned to crochet and made scarves for myself, my mother-in-law, and Yasmine, as well as a baby blanket for a friend who had become a new mom.

I finally began using the fancy bathtub that I insisted on having, but never got around to using. I briefly revisited my "atta-girl" box to remind myself of all the great things I had accomplished. I looked at old photos to remind myself of my own "badassery." I blew bubbles, sent coloring books to a grieving friend, and became a life member of my sorority. I sent a new set of my favorite bedsheets to Tina and Miko, along with a love letter. I watched an incredible video on how to freeze a bubble, sent to me by a friend, and created my annual vision board.

My sixty-by-sixty campaign was one of the most challenging, exhilarating, and life-changing experiences of my life. The finale was an amazing surprise sixtieth birthday party coordinated by my amazing husband and attended live and virtually by over a hundred of the people I hold most dear. At sixty years old, I took inventory of my life and realized I was settled and content with every aspect of my life.

And then I had to say farewell to Mom. As I close out my story, it feels only fitting to reflect upon the most significant influence in my life, just as I did when I began my story. The most challenging aspect of writing this book has been addressing and depicting the complex relationship I had with my mother. It is a topic that stirs a multitude of emotions within me, emotions that are difficult to put into words.

The holiday season of 2022 was a bittersweet one for our family, when we were first forced to grapple with the heartbreaking news that Mom had lung cancer. Because of the location of the mass, as well as my mom's fragile constitution, neither surgery, chemotherapy nor radiation were options for her. We simply had to monitor her health and make her as comfortable as possible.

Witnessing this remarkable woman undergoing rapid, profound changes made 2023 very hard on my siblings and me. At eighty-eight years old, Mom remained strong, but her body sometimes failed to cooperate with her. Throughout her entire life, she had been adamant about maintaining a sense of independence. Watching her become less mobile and seeing the toll it took on her was tough. We also noted a shift in her personality.

Though Mom didn't live with us, I was reminded that the role I assumed at a young age as a parental figure still stood. Employing a firmer tone with my mother had proven effective when necessary. My niece, with whom my mother lived during this past year, playfully joked that she would report to me when my mother stepped out of line.

As her illness progressed, my mother's changing personality eventually reached a point where our conversations no longer evoked the same response as they used to. I had to constantly remind myself that with dementia setting in, Mom was not the same woman who raised me, nor was she the mom I had known all these years. It was a sobering realization. I was keenly aware that my time with Mom was limited and so did the best I could to spend time with her whenever I could and make her final chapter on earth as comfortable and peaceful as possible.

If I am honest, I must admit that I harbored an unconscious hope that as my mother aged, she would mellow and find tranquility. Unfortunately, with the numerous ailments she faced, the opposite occurred. I therefore had to make a conscious effort to pray before talking with her in person or on the phone. Doing this allowed me to maintain composure and manage my own emotions.

Throughout the years, I have come to accept that my mother was not equipped to provide me with the emotional support and reinforcement I needed. My adult life has been an ongoing process of reconciling my expectations and recognizing the limitations that have influenced our relationship. This realization has been both liberating and bittersweet.

Simultaneously, I find solace in the relationships I have cultivated with women of my mother's generation. These incredible women have had profoundly positive impacts on my life, serving as beacons of guidance, wisdom, and support. Their influence has been invaluable, and I am grateful for the lessons imparted to me.

However, their presence and the gifts they brought could not and cannot fill the void that remained in my relationship with my mother. There was a deep yearning within me for a connection that was probably unrealistic for me to have. I continually prayed to find my peace with it. There is no doubt in my mind that my mom did the very best she could. I also know I wasn't the easiest daughter to raise.

Over her final months, there were some scary moments when we feared we might lose her. I prayed to have the wisdom to know when I needed to be there with her. On the Monday before her passing, after a sad afternoon when all four of her children were gathered with her via Zoom, my spirit told me to get in the car and go to her.

While I appreciated technology giving us the ability to be with her virtually, I needed to be with her and touch her. That evening, I drove the five and a half hours from my door to hers without stopping.

Once I arrived, I was so grateful for my decision to drop everything and go to her. As it turned out that Monday night would be the last time Mom would speak.

My niece and namesake and I were sitting on Mom's bed. I asked Mom if she knew who I was and she loudly and proudly, replied, "Barbara JoAnn Lee." Feeling both sad and immensely grateful, I struggled to fight back tears. Mom then started vigorously chanting, "Nam-Myoho-Renge-Kyo."

Little Barbara and I have made it a running joke in trying to figure out to whom she was directing her final words, and what they meant. My niece is a Muslim, so I have a feeling Mom was talking to me she said:

"Get a beautiful dress, show a little booty."

My siblings arrived the next day, and my siblings, niece and nephew all spent the week together. It was the first time we were all under the same roof in decades. We bonded over food, Netflix, and shared funny stories. Because the house was so full, I decided to sleep in Mom's bed with her the next night. As the nurse told us the end was near, I was afraid I'd wake up and she would be dead.

I spent nearly all night checking on her breathing. Though Mom never said another word, she moved around and kicked all night. I think she was signaling to me she wanted her bed back to herself. (chuckle)

Three days later, Mom died peacefully in her sleep.

Though we knew it was coming, my heart shattered into a million pieces. One part of me was relieved that she was no longer suffering. And she had said her goodbyes. That relief didn't last that long. The other part of me was devastated at the finality of it all.

In sharing these thoughts and reflections, I am reminded of the inherent complexity of human relationships, particularly those with our parents. It is a blend of love, longing, acceptance, and unfulfilled desires that coexist within the depths of our souls.

I will always carry a deep appreciation for the many, many lessons learned and the resilience fostered through this intricate bond I uniquely held with my mom. For the next few weeks, I poured my energy into planning a send-off befitting of this amazing woman.

Mom's memorial was a true celebration of the phenomenal, strong and beloved woman she was. Buddhist members, family and friends came from all over to say their farewells. Mom would have been very happy with her send-off.

So how do I carry on Mom's amazing legacy? Out of Mom's four children, I believe I am the one who has most fully embraced the Asian side of my heritage. I am hopeful that my continued embracing of Japanese culture, philosophies and life approaches, will somehow contribute to keeping her legacy alive.

My children were the only ones she insisted on calling her Obachan, — grandmother in Japanese. I'm so glad she did, and I now want my grandchildren to call me Obachan. My oldest brother named all his children after family members. Two of them are named after Mom. One has the male version of her first name, a second has her last name. I love that he honored Mom in this way.

During one of Mom's moves, we lost her families' contact information. We should have taken better care of that information, as we now have no easy way of finding Mom's relatives. I worry that as we get further removed from our Asian ancestry, we will be further removed from that our connection. I wish I had a connection to Mom's family and am committed to researching to find this other half of our family. It is important to me to keep Mom's legacy alive.

Happiness is a Verb.
And a Journey.

As I approach the conclusion of this book, I find myself reflecting on a statement made by a former anchor who made a remark about women being past their primes after the age of forty. I recently reflected on celebrating yet another birthday well beyond my fortieth, while simultaneously finally completing my lifelong dream of sharing my story. Perhaps, according to his definition, I am indeed past my prime.

However, had I written this book during what he deems my prime, I would not have accumulated the multitude of lessons, made the necessary mistakes, nor experienced the enlightening epiphanies that have shaped me into who I am today. For all of this, I am profoundly grateful.

What is my biggest lesson? What may appear glittery isn't always gold. If you're this close to the end of this book, you'll likely have shaken your head multiple times and formed judgments about me. And that's perfectly fine. That reaction aligns with my goal— to emphasize that there's so much more beneath the surface than meets the eye.

While I often claim I don't like change, the reality is that throughout my entire life, change has been my only constant, and the future promises to be no different. As I brace myself and work toward embracing even more change, there are several daily "non-negotiables" that I will continue to uphold. I will keep my faith at the center of my life. I will nourish my body with wholesome choices. I'll continue to surround myself with positive influences and focus on cultivating optimism and uplifting others. I am committed to prioritizing consistent physical and mental exercise. I will vigorously safeguard my spirit by being selective about the energies I allow into my life.

I'll never again struggle with my identity, nor question where I fit in. I've defined my own place, established my own standards, and have a sense of freedom that I have in fact, cultivated.

My hope is that you, by now hopefully my friend, will continue to seek and embrace change, for there is an abundance of extraordinary experiences awaiting you beyond the confines of our comfort zone. So what does this all mean? I am grateful to have lived this amazing, authentic very human experience called life, and I have not one single regret. I would not have chosen to do anything different, even with all my foibles, missteps, mistakes and challenges.

I'm hopeful that out of this journey thus far you've captured a balanced picture of a very flawed, but authentic person whose primary hope is to, in some small way, help and inspire others.

When I deeply reflect on the moments in my life when I felt the most empowered, several instances stand out: my first day as a freshman at Penn State, the experience of beginning graduate school, the sheer joy of becoming a mother, successfully navigating corporate America, my scary but exhilarating leap into entrepreneurship, and now the amazing feeling that surges through me as I approach completion of this book.

Despite their distinctiveness, what do all of these milestones share in common? Each represents key defining points in my personal growth and self-discovery. They each are a result of my stepping outside of my comfort zone and embracing uncertainty and new challenges.

And each of these instances of self-empowerment were fueled by my deep sense of purpose and passion. I am absolutely convinced that I can tackle any challenge and overcome any obstacle.

I am filled with gratitude for my family, friends, sisters, brothers, and all who have been a part of my lifelong journey. Indeed, I am that graceful swan gliding effortlessly on the water, while fully embracing the flapping under the surface. My entire support system sits just below that surface and has held me up.

People say that life is short. But I say life is long. As such, it is a day-by-day, effort-by-effort, and decision-by-decision journey. In answer to the question of whether I am ever satisfied? I can confidently say that my response is no. Am I more comfortable sitting still and just "being" now? I'd respond with a resounding yes.

My commitment to change and self-improvement is lifelong. I am constantly embarking on transformative journeys. In September of 2022, inspired by my longtime friend Kandii Saddler-Moore, Michael and I made the conscious decision to drastically change our eating habits and take more control over our health. We eliminated carbs and sugar from our diet and increased our physical activity. The result? We successfully shed the weight we'd gained during quarantine, and we immediately felt so much better.

Though it's a constant challenge and we sometimes fall off, both Michael and I have remained determined to maintain our joint commitment to our health. Though I do not deprive myself of anything, embracing clean eating has been a game-changer. I also continue to prioritize sleep hygiene and proactively manage my overall health daily.

Barb Lee Gee Lee Pratt is continually evolving. I am *"nearly-totally"* comfortable with myself. Am I still nervous before a big presentation, upon meeting new people, and in certain situations? Yes.

But do I feel like I am enough? Always.

Where my ability to heal has shown up most is in my wide range of great friendships with women and men alike. I am fortunate to say I have an unusually large number of close friends. I mean real close friends. A lot of them. I share myself, and I truly value each friendship. I also adopted a lot of moms and mother figures along the way. They all know who they are. I am immensely grateful for them all. I sincerely believe I have the best relationships in the world and appreciate how lucky I am.

The reality is that the key to finding the right person is striving to be the best person we can be. Most of what we have in our lives is a reflection back to us of what we give. After years of attempting to please some, I no longer feel the need to do so. Instead of investing my time, energy, and spirit into relationships in which I am unsure of my place, I choose to focus on the individuals who sow into me. I'm referring to those who seek to understand me, listen to me, and who "get" me, as much as I "get" them.

When you find your true people, you know it, and they know it! Let others do with their energy what they must. My goal is to conserve mine and use it for good.

Accepting that I am not perfect absolves me of the responsibility of trying to be perfect. I've discovered that life became easier when I decided to allow people to make assumptions and potentially misunderstand me. It's too hard trying to understand how people feel about me and then figuring out ways to dispel any "untruths." How people experience me is part of their truths. It's real for them, and that's okay.

I aspire to love people where they are, not where I am. Give them what they communicate that they need, rather than what we feel most comfortable giving.

I mentioned earlier that our circumstances play a significant role in shaping who we are. However, my Buddhist teachings emphasize that our attitude or mindset is what truly determines whether we experience happiness or misery. I'm not suggesting that thinking happy thoughts alone will make us happy. Rather, we have the power to change how we perceive and respond to things. It is not our spouse's or partner's responsibility to make us happy. Happiness is a state of mind for which we are accountable. It comes from within.

I don't have all the answers on how to attain happiness. What I do know is a sure-fire path to unhappiness is when we train our mindset to turn everything into an issue. Instead of wearing rose-colored glasses, if we view life through jaded lenses, we will find exactly what we're looking for.

Being in quarantine for so long helped me to recognize my strong need for solitude, increased family time, and the importance of nurturing relationships that return the care and support I give. The experience of quarantine also revealed aspects of my personality that I had not before fully grasped. I am, to a greater extent than I'd ever thought, an introvert.

For those who knew me in my youth or have been around me for any length of time, this revelation may come as a surprise. The truth is, I am still in the process of defining what brings me comfort and contentment, and I no longer feel compelled to conform to external pressures. I've already been around the block with marriage (two great husbands) two amazing young men to whom I gave birth, three great bonus children, even some cool bonus grandchildren, as well as all that other stuff, professional career, etc. What is more important now? The peace I can experience on a Friday night from doing absolutely nothing. And yes, my profession allows me to wear "cool, chic clothing and comfortable shoes."

I believe my life's body of work speaks for itself, and that was why it was so important for me to share my story. Hopefully, these are lessons and some epiphanies that inspire you to take chances, push yourself beyond fear, and shoot way beyond the stars!

I don't fully know what this next phase of my life holds, but I do know, that I'm committed to doing what Mom told me:

I'm surely gonna get some beautiful dresses, and you can bet that I'm gonna show some booty!

Sources

Barnett, B., & Parker, G. (1998). The parentified child: Early competence or childhood deprivation. Child Psychology and Psychiatry Review, 3(4).

Brown, Helen Gurley (1982) Having It All. New York: Simon & Schuster

Goff, Bob. Twitter, October 2014

Holmes, Oliver Wendell. Dan Miller Quotes, 2024

Koren, Leonard (2008)Wabi-Sabi for Artists, Designers, Poets & Philosophers: California: Imperfect Publishing

Sotomayor, Sonia (2013) My Beloved World. New York: Vintage

Made in the USA
Columbia, SC
03 June 2024

23c516cf-fa7a-4609-8b56-b9996da547d8R01